colate & vanilla choc
e & vanilla chocolate
colate & vanilla choc
vanilla chocolate & va
te & vanilla chocolat
illa chocolate & vani
olate & vanilla choco
e & vanilla chocolate
anilla chocolate & va
ocolate & vanilla ch
anilla chocolate & va
te & vanilla chocolat
nilla chocolate & va

lla chocolate & vanilla choco

Also by Gale Gand

chocolate & vanilla

gale gand with Lisa Weiss

Clarkson Potter/Publishers

New York

Published in the United States by Clarkson Potter/Publishers,
an imprint of the Crown Publishing Group,
a division of Random House, Inc., New York.
www.crownpublishing.com
www.clarksonpotter.com

Clarkson N. Potter is a trademark and Potter and colophon
are registered trademarks of Random House, Inc.

Library of Congress Cataloging-in-Publication Data
Gand, Gale.
    Chocolate and vanilla / Gale Gand with Lisa Weiss.
      p.   cm.
1. Cookery (Chocolate).   2. Cookery (Vanilla).   I. Weiss, Lisa, 1951–   II. Title.
TX767.C5G36   2006
641.6'374—dc22   2006002988

ISBN-13: 978-0-307-23852-8
ISBN-10: 0-307-23852-0

Printed in the United States of America

Design by Laura Palese

10   9   8   7   6   5   4   3   2   1

First Edition

This book is dedicated to my darling family: my sweet, loving husband, Jimmy Seidita; son, Gio Gand Tramonto; and new, twin daughters, Ella and Ruby Gand Seidita, who were kicking inside of me as I started writing this book. You all give me a reason to cook and bake and I love it. Thank you for making my life the one I dreamt of having.

chocolate

ocolatechocolatechocolatechocolatechocolatechocolatecho
nocolatechocolatechocolatechocolatechocolatechocolatech

DARK (BITTERSWEET) CHOCOLATE

SEMI-SWEET CHOCOLATE

techocolatechocolatechocolatechocolatechocolatechocolat
latechocolatechocolatechocolatechocolatechocolatechocola

LIGHT AND MILK CHOCOLATE

WHITE CHOCOLATE

Introduction to Chocolate

Many people see things in terms of black and white, but I always seem to see things in terms of chocolate and vanilla. Maybe that's because the first important decision I can remember making had to do with choosing between chocolate or vanilla at Tastee-Freez.

Whenever Chicago's summer heat and humidity became too much to bear, my mother, brother, and I would tumble into my father's Thunderbird convertible and go to cool ourselves with soft-serve ice cream cones on the Tastee-Freez patio. In the late 1950s, soft-serve ice cream—a kind of frozen custard—was popular at many drive-ins, but we thought Tastee-Freez's was the absolute best. There were only two flavors, and in my five-year-old mind I remember thinking my personality would be forever defined by my choice. Was I a "golden girl"? or a "chocolate chick"?—a decision made all the more difficult because not only did I have to state publicly which flavor I wanted, but then I had to choose between dips: vanilla butterscotch "angel dip" or chocolate "devil dip." Was I going to follow my big brother's lead and go with chocolate all the way, or assert my independence with all vanilla? It then occurred to me that I could just play the middle and choose vanilla ice cream with a devil dip.

After twenty years as a professional pastry chef, I *still* haven't decided whether I'm a chocolate chick or a golden girl, but I *have* come to the conclusion that most people are one or the other. Even as you read this I'll bet you've already decided which camp you're in—and which camp your friends and loved ones fall into as well.

I wrote this book to pay homage to America's two favorite flavors, to share some of the chocolate and vanilla recipes that mean the most to me and that I really love to make, and to help indulge the chocolate and vanilla lovers in your lives.

There's more than a good chance that there's an ardent chocoholic in your close circle, because while vanilla reigned as America's queen flavor for almost two hundred years, now chocolate is king and even seems to be gaining in popularity. At Tru, the fine-

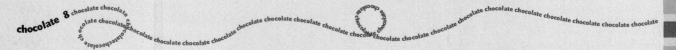

dining restaurant in Chicago I co-own and where I work as an executive pastry chef, I love going into the dining room and asking guests to let me choose desserts for their table. I begin by asking them if they're chocolate people or custard people (*custard* being just a code word for vanilla). Without question, the chocolate people make up a very vocal and emphatic majority—"Bring on the five-course chocolate collection!"—and I'm always happy to oblige.

As a pastry chef, I've always known that understanding the history of and working with chocolate is like acquiring a much-needed second language: You can live with knowing just the basics of Chocolate 101, or keep going for your PhD. My knowledge fell somewhere in between until a few years ago when I took my whole Tru pastry staff to a lecture about the history of chocolate at the Field Museum in Chicago given by Michael Coe, author (with Sophie D. Coe) of *The True History of Chocolate*. I had what I like to call my "chocolate mini-epiphany." I realized I wanted to learn more about this ingredient I was holding in my hands and working with every day. What is *so* magical about chocolate that it elicits *so* much passion, *so* much joy, and *so* much pleasure?

The intriguing historical saga of the cacao bean begins deep in the tropical forests of the New World, where the bean was once ground into a paste by hand to make a sacred drink for the Mayans and Aztecs. Next it travels to the New World where cacao became the favorite beverage in the royal courts of Europe; and then finally the story brings us to today, where chocolate is one of the world's most popular flavors and is manufactured using sophisticated technology based on ancient methods. (I'm still amazed, even after making chocolate myself, that crunchy beans tediously and laboriously ground over and over again with sugar can be transformed into unctuously smooth and sublime chocolate.) Now every time I take a bite of chocolate, I appreciate it even more than before.

I hope that knowing just a little about the history of chocolate will increase your own chocolate appreciation, even if you're simply sneaking a few chocolate chips as you make your next batch of cookie dough. But what I *really* hope is that you'll be in the kitchen making one of the recipes from this book. Second only to the pleasure I get from seeing the delight on someone's face as they take a bite of one of my desserts, is sharing the recipe for that dessert and knowing they'll go home, make it, and share that delight with people they love.

The chocolate recipes I've chosen for this book are all about memories—memories past and memories in the making. The ones I put in my "memories past" file include updated versions of childhood favorites, such as s'mores and Twinkies (Chocolate Fudge Soccer Cakes), and recipes I've been making for years at Tru and that guests are always asking for, such as Best-Ever Fudgy Brownies and Milk Chocolate Star Anise Crème Brûlée Spoonfuls. Then there are the recipes in my "memories-in-the-making" file, which are those I like to imagine a child requesting over and over again for special occasions or afternoon treats: maybe Cream Cheese–Stuffed Chocolate Cupcakes, or Chocolate-Praline Cake in a Jar.

I've organized the recipes by flavor—dark, semi-sweet, milk, or white chocolate— because that's the way I personally like to approach what kind of dessert I'm going to make. Rather than look for a cake or cookie recipe, if it's chocolate I'm in the mood for, I think: Do I want a rich, dark grown-up chocolate flavor, like the Mexican Hot Chocolate Fondue or Guanaja Sherbet, or do I want something a little lighter and not so bitter, maybe something that will appeal to kids, like the Hot Fudge Sundaes?

The majority of the recipes can be easily and quickly put together, such as Cocoa "Cup" Cakes and Deep Chocolate Shortbread, but a couple, such as Chocolate Crêpes Filled with Chocolate Mousse and Chocolate Babka, you'll probably want to save for a rainy afternoon. While these two may be time-consuming, they still conform to my unwritten rule that a recipe should never be technically difficult or require hard-to-find ingredients. All the recipes I've included here I make myself—at home, that is.

Because I know how precious time can be these days (with three kids under age ten, boy, do I know!) with carpools to be driven and late nights at work, I've included do-

ahead tips at the end of each recipe. You'll also find notes on any special equipment you'll need, such as cake pans (and what size) or a candy thermometer or parchment paper, so you can get everything organized in advance.

Enough already. Go and take that bar of chocolate out of the pantry and make a batch of brownies. Create some memories.

A Brief History of the Cacao Bean

When the icy winter winds are howling off Lake Michigan in Chicago, nothing lifts my spirits and warms my soul like a cup of rich, dark, and foamy Mexican hot chocolate, lightly sweetened and spiced with hints of cinnamon. With each sip I think about the origins of this drink that was so beloved by the ancient Maya and Aztecs. Even to this day, it's not uncommon to find people in parts of central and southern Mexico still routinely drinking hot chocolate, just as their ancestors did before them, although the Mexican hot chocolate drunk today bears little resemblance to the bitter beverage flavored with chilies and spices made by the Maya and Aztecs.

Although archaeologists think it was the Olmecs (1500 to 400 BC) who were the first people to eat the fruit of the cacao (ka-*kow*) tree, the Maya (AD 250 to 900) were the first to figure out how to harvest, ferment, roast, and grind the cacao beans into a paste that could be thinned out with water and cornmeal to make a drink. Carl Linnaeus, the eighteenth-century botanist (and an admitted chocoholic), heard of the Mayan belief that the cacao tree was a gift to them from the gods and gave it its Greek botanical name, *Theobroma,* or "food of the gods."

Use of the cacao bean spread from the Maya to the Aztecs, who worshipped the cacao bean for the power they believed it possessed to give a man superhuman strength and endurance, both on the battlefield and—ahem!—in the bedroom. They served it at banquets and religious rites and used it as a drug, a food, and even as currency—one bean for a tomato, ten beans for a rabbit, one hundred for a slave—because it was more valuable to them than gold. (Gold was everywhere, cacao trees weren't; and the Aztecs depended on tribes they conquered to grow the trees for them.) To make the bitter drink a little tastier they blended the cacao paste with flavorings such as chilies, allspice, and vanilla, and then would toss the liquid back and forth between two vessels until it frothed, believing that the spirit of the drink was found in the foam.

Spaniard Hernando Cortés, who conquered the Aztecs in 1519, was the first European to "discover" chocolate as a beverage, because Columbus had missed the boat, literally. In 1502, on Columbus's third voyage to the New World, he found a stash of cacao beans in a Mayan canoe, but he thought the beans were just some strange form of Aztec money and didn't realize their value as something edible.

When Cortés arrived in Mexico, Emperor Montezuma II mistook him for an exiled god-king and welcomed the Spaniard with a big banquet. After dinner Montezuma served the honored guest his favorite beverage—hot chocolate, of course—then proceeded to throw in a few cacao plantations as a gift. Cortés, who was aware of the value the Aztecs placed on cacao beans, slyly started cashing the beans from his trees in for gold. By the time Montezuma was wise to the fact that the avaricious conquistador wasn't a god and was really only after his gold, it was too late. Cortés had the emperor thrown in jail, where Montezuma died, cacao-less and humiliated, in 1520.

Cortés took cacao beans back to Spain, but the bitter chocolate drink he made with the beans was not too well received—that is, until someone (probably Cortés) sweetened the drink with sugar to make it more palatable. Soon hot chocolate was all the rage among sixteenth-century Spanish nobility, and aristocratic ladies could be seen daintily sipping the beverage morning, noon, and night.

By the eighteenth century the exotic New World ingredient could be seen all over Europe and in the American colonies, but because the beans were still being laboriously

ground by hand, the price of chocolate was still out of reach for most people. Then something happened that altered the course of chocolate history forever: In 1728 Walter Churchman built the first water-powered chocolate mill in Bristol, England, and gradually—although it was still considered a luxury—chocolate became more available to everyone.

The nineteenth century brought about a new era of chocolate production (you'll recognize some of these names): In 1828 Dutchman Conrad Van Houten created the world's first cocoa powder by separating out the cocoa butter from the ground beans (called *mass*), grinding the mass to a powder, and then adding an alkalai to make it less acidic—what we call Dutch-processed cocoa. Then in 1874 Rudolphe Lindt invented a machine, which is still used today, that mixes, or *conches,* cacao paste (also called cocoa liquor) with cocoa butter, sugar, and flavorings into a smooth liquid for molding. A couple of years later Swiss inventors Daniel Peter and Henri Nestlé figured out a way to combine conched chocolate with condensed milk, creating—you guessed it—milk chocolate. Soon chocolate became more like the stuff we know today: sweet, smooth, and shaped into bars.

In the twentieth century, entrepreneurs such as John Cadbury, Domingo Ghirardelli, Etienne Guittard, and, most prominently, Milton Hershey brought us even more sophisticated techniques for transforming cacao beans into smooth molded bars of chocolate for eating and baking. The companies they founded have since become household names.

Today, the annual worldwide consumption of chocolate is a whopping sixty billion pounds. From supermarket shelves, upscale confectioners, or by mail order, whether you're buying chocolate for baking or eating out of hand, you have more choices than ever before; and, luckily for all of the world's chocolate lovers, chocolate's history is still being written.

From Bean to Bar How Chocolate Is Made

Cacao trees grow in rain forests in a global belt that extends roughly twenty degrees north and south of the equator. The fruit pods, looking kind of like elongated tough-skinned melons (or deflated colorful footballs, if you're a sports fan), hang directly from the trunks of the cacao trees. Each pod contains an average of thirty to fifty almond-shaped seeds, or beans, snugly nestled in a sweet but tangy white pulp. When cut open, the ripe pods release the powerful aroma of chocolate.

"You say cocoa, I say cacao."—Generally you use cacao (*ka-kow*) when referring to the tree or its beans, and cocoa (*ko-ko*) when you are talking about the products from the beans, such as cocoa powder and cocoa butter.

Once the ripe pods have been harvested by hand, the beans are carefully removed, still with a little of the pulp clinging to them, and the first—and some think the most crucial—stage in the process begins. The grayish-white beans are put into boxes or earthen pits, covered with banana leaves, and allowed to ferment in order to develop flavor, aroma, and color as their sugars turn into acids, in a process similar to making wine from grapes.

After the approximate week-long fermentation, the now russet-colored beans are dried for ten to twenty days, sometimes on trays in the sun, or if the climate is particularly humid, in heated indoor rooms. After drying, they're sorted by size and shipped to factories all over the world, but mainly in Europe and the United States.

At the factory the fermented and dried beans are roasted for thirty minutes to two hours and at temperatures from 210°F to 300°F, depending on the type of bean, and then are quickly cooled. Roasting causes the hardened outer shells of the beans to crack and fall off, revealing the good stuff: the nibs. The cocoa nibs, or the edible "meat" of the cacao bean, are about fifty percent fat. The process of turning the nibs into chocolate begins

with grinding them in a series of mechanical rollers. The friction from the rolling creates heat that causes the nibs to liquefy and separate into two masses: one a smooth paste that's called chocolate liquor (not something alcoholic but packed with bitter chocolate flavor) and the other, liquid fat, the cocoa butter.

It's at this stage that the chocolate liquor can be turned into either cocoa or chocolate for eating or baking. If the cocoa butter is removed almost completely, the remaining chocolate liquor can be further refined until it becomes cocoa powder (there's only a trace of fat in cocoa powder), the process Van Houten invented (see page 13). If the chocolate liquor is ground further and then sloshed back and forth with the addition of cocoa butter in a process called *conching*, the resulting mass can be made into chocolate bars. In *conching*, chocolate liquor is heated, ground, and blended with cocoa butter (and sometimes sugar and milk powder) in a large machine (that originally resembled a conch shell) to remove any graininess. The process can take anywhere from twelve hours to three days, depending on the quality of the chocolate desired: Fine chocolates are conched longer to get a smoother texture and better balance of flavor.

Chocolate destined for chocolate bars or molding then has to undergo *tempering*, in which the conched liquid goes through a precise process of heating and cooling to stabilize the fat crystals in the emulsified cocoa butter to give it a mirror-like sheen and crisp snap when broken. Tempered chocolate also doesn't melt when touched by warm hands. Once the tempered chocolate has been formed into bars or bonbons, it's cooled, unmolded, and then wrapped and shipped.

Buying Chocolate

Even *I* have trouble deciding what to buy when faced with the huge array of chocolates on my local market's baking shelf. It used to be enough to call chocolate unsweetened, bittersweet, semi-sweet, or milk chocolate. Now there are bars labeled with percentages of cacao and place of origin, not to mention specifics like "fair trade" and "organic." There are chips and bars, pistoles of course, but also blocks, coins, shavings, and nibs. What's a girl to choose?

The main thing to keep in mind is that when you see a percentage of cacao listed on the label, it indicates the percentage of chocolate liquor in proportion to sugar. It has nothing to do with the percentage of cocoa butter and other ingredients such as lecithin (a natural emulsifier that binds the ingredients together and makes the chocolate smooth), dry milk powder, or vanilla that also may have been added. Basically, the higher the proportion of cacao, the darker the color, less sweet the taste, and stronger the chocolate flavor of the finished chocolate.

Many manufacturers have started labeling their chocolates by bean. Three varieties of cacao trees produce the majority of beans destined for the chocolate-making process. They are the criollo, forestero, and trinitario. The criollo bean is the most prized because it has the best balance of fruitiness with acidity. Forestero trees yield the largest number of beans and account for the bulk of the world's production of chocolate, about ninety percent. Trinitario trees are a cross between the forestero and criollo and combine the best of both: heartiness and flavor.

Some chocolates are also now labeled by place of origin, the place where the cocoa trees are grown. One example is Valrhona's Guanaja, named after Guanaja Island, off the coast of Honduras, where the beans are grown exclusively. Guanaja chocolate is very intense and dark with a seventy-percent cacao content. It's made from a blend of criollo and trinitario beans and has a delicate, nutty, coffee-like flavor. Valrhona's Guanaja is one of the few brands I recommend by name in this book. In addition there are several organic manufacturers who adhere to strict guidelines concerning the use of pesticides and chemicals and are actively involved in promoting the sustainability of the rain forests.

All that said, for this book I decided to keep things simple and have divided the recipes into dark (bittersweet) chocolate, semi-sweet chocolate (including chips or unsweetened or cocoa powder combined with sugar), light and milk chocolate, and white chocolate. Here are some general guidelines to use when shopping for chocolate:

UNSWEETENED, BITTER, OR BAKING CHOCOLATE

Just as its name implies, unsweetened chocolate has no sugar. That's why it tastes bitter and is not something you'd want to sneak a bite of in the middle of the night. The percentage of cacao (chocolate liquor) is 100 percent, although sometimes it has a little vanilla or lecithin added.

BITTERSWEET AND SEMI-SWEET CHOCOLATE

This is the category of chocolate that is the most confusing because manufacturers use the terms *bittersweet* and *semi-sweet* interchangeably, but the bottom line is that your taste buds are the boss. To be labeled either as bittersweet or semi-sweet in the United States, a chocolate must contain a minimum of thirty-five percent cacao solids, but most contain anywhere from fifty-two percent to seventy-two percent cacao solids—the amount depends on the manufacturer. For me, bittersweet chocolate has more of a "dark chocolate" flavor, and semi-sweet has less chocolate flavor. So if a recipe calls for semi-sweet and you like your chocolate with a "darker" flavor, use one that is labeled bittersweet or one that has a higher percentage of cacao solids, as it contains less sugar.

COCOA POWDER

I use a lot of cocoa powder in my recipes because it not only brings intense chocolate flavor to a recipe but is easy to measure and mix. Dutch-processed cocoa powder has been treated with an alkali (usually potassium carbonate) to neutralize its acidity. It has a mellower flavor and is easier to dissolve in liquids than "un-Dutched" cocoa. In my recipes I specify Dutch-processed when it's important to the outcome; otherwise I just say "cocoa powder" and you can use either.

MILK CHOCOLATE

Milk solids (at least twelve percent) are added to the chocolate liquor (a minimum of ten percent) to create a very smooth, soft, almost chewy chocolate, the choice of most children. This is the chocolate usually used in the kind of candy bars you get at Halloween (okay, I'll admit they're the ones I like to give out so I'll have them left over). The best have a wonderful but subtle caramel flavor from the milk.

WHITE CHOCOLATE

It seems people either love it or hate it but no matter, white chocolate is not really chocolate at all because it contains no cacao. It's a blend of cocoa butter and sugar and sometimes butterfat, milk solids, lecithin, and vanilla. I like white chocolate best when it's combined with other ingredients, particularly toasted nuts or citrus flavors.

GIANDUJA CHOCOLATE

Developed in Switzerland, Gianduja (pronounced *john-doo-ya*) is one of my favorites. It is milk or dark chocolate blended with praline paste made from toasted and ground hazelnuts to create a seriously smooth, nutty-tasting soft chocolate.

CHOCOLATE NIBS

Extracted after roasting, nibs are the edible meat of the cocoa bean. I don't call for cocoa nibs in any of these recipes but they're a fun way to get some crunchy texture into a dish along with some chocolate flavor. They're great folded into homemade vanilla ice cream or sprinkled on other desserts. Nibs are sold mostly in tins and are small shavings from the roasted beans.

CHOCOLATE CHIPS AND PISTOLES

Chocolate chips, which are made with less cocoa butter than chocolate bars, were designed solely to retain their shape when baked in a dessert—think Toll House cookies —and shouldn't be substituted in recipes calling for chopped and melted chocolate. They also tend to be sweeter and have less chocolate flavor. On the other hand, disk- or

coin-shaped *pistoles* (also called *callets, pastilles,* and *buttons*) are made of the same high-quality dark chocolate found in bars, and are designed specifically for melting. Pistoles are available from specialty markets and by mail order (see Sources, page 79). Lately I've also been able to buy good-quality chocolate already cut into chunks or chips for ease of use.

COUVERTURE CHOCOLATE

Couverture, or "covering," chocolate is dark chocolate that has at least thirty-two percent cocoa butter added to make it especially glossy and smooth, perfect for thinly coating candies and bonbons with a shell that has extra snap when cracked open. It's used primarily by pastry chefs and confectioners and is not readily available, although many premium brands of chocolate, such as Valrhona, have enough cocoa butter to be considered "couverture." Couverture chocolate should not be confused with confectionary coating (also called compound coating), which is a blend of vegetable fats with sugar and cocoa powder (some cheap brands even include paraffin). It barely resembles real chocolate in either texture or flavor.

Working with Chocolate

For most of the recipes in this book I don't ask you to do anything too tricky (no tempering called for here), but there are a few basics you should know, particularly if you are new to working with chocolate.

STORING CHOCOLATE

You finally managed to decide at the store what chocolate to buy and you bring it home. Now what? People are always asking me if they can store chocolate in the freezer and the answer is no. Once you take it out of the freezer, or even the fridge, it can attract moisture from the air, causing condensation to form on the chocolate and creating the possibility that it might seize when you try to melt it (see Melting Chocolate, below). Always keep your chocolate well wrapped in plastic or in an airtight bag or container to prevent it from absorbing any other flavors or odors, and store it in a cool (60 to 70 degrees F), dry place such as the pantry or a cupboard. Just don't leave it there too long —a year is too long—or the chocolate may bloom and/or lose flavor. (Can you tell that to my husband, please? He's always hoarding good chocolate and then by the time he surrenders to it, it's past its prime.) The "bloom" or white dusty-looking streaks that sometimes form on a piece of chocolate are just the fats or cocoa butter moving to the surface. Bloom is usually caused by too much heat or moisture during storage and while it's not harmful, it's a sign the chocolate has begun to deteriorate.

MEASURING CHOCOLATE

Most recipes call for chocolate in ounces rather than in cups (chocolate chips are the exception) because this is how the chocolate is sold. Many bars come divided into squares to make measuring easy; for example, unsweetened baking chocolate comes in eight-ounce bars divided into eight one-ounce squares. A kitchen scale is great for measuring out the chunks, either before or after you chop them.

CHOPPING CHOCOLATE

The best way I've found to chop chocolate, whether it's to speed up the melting process (small pieces melt faster than large chunks) or just to have shavings for sprinkling on a pie for garnish, is to use a high-quality, large serrated knife, the kind you'd use to slice a large loaf of crusty bread. Place the block or bar of chocolate on a cutting board, tuck your fingers under for safety, and just cut down, almost as if you're trying to slice it thin, and the chocolate will break off into little shards or splinters.

MAKING CHOCOLATE CURLS

To make beautiful curls of chocolate for decorating desserts, the two keys are to use a block of chocolate and have it at barely above room temperature. If it's too cold it will break into shards as you peel it. At the restaurant we leave the chocolate block near or over a warm oven. At home you could warm it with a hair dryer set on low, or try

wrapping it in a tea towel and warming it with the heat of your hands. Use a vegetable peeler and pull across the side of the block so the chocolate comes off in curls. Place them on a plate and refrigerate until you need them.

MELTING CHOCOLATE

I put the chopped chocolate in a metal or glass bowl and place the bowl over a saucepan of simmering water to create a double boiler, or *bain-marie* as we call it at the restaurant. (If you happen to own a standard double boiler, by all means use it!) I stir the chocolate occasionally with a rubber spatula, making sure no water or condensation gets into the melting chocolate because water could cause it to stiffen or "seize." If that happens the chocolate almost never recovers. Because white chocolate is temperamental when it comes to melting and can scorch or clump up easily, have the water a little cooler than for other chocolates; less than just barely simmering should do the trick. Some people like to melt chocolate in their microwave . . . but I'm not one of those people. I feel like I can't see what's going on and I could easily scorch or burn the chocolate without realizing it until it's too late. Chocolate's way too expensive for me to take the chance of ruining it and maybe—just maybe—I'm a bit of a control freak. (But a really nice control freak.)

best-ever fudgy **brownies**

MAKES ABOUT FOUR DOZEN 2-INCH BROWNIES

Super moist and fudgy—not at all cake-like—these brownies are so thin that they're really half brownie and half frosting. At Tru, I serve them as petits fours—one- or two-bite pieces for after dessert—because the chocolate flavor is really intense, but at home you can cut them any size you'd like. As a rule, I don't like to recommend a specific brand of chocolate, but I love the taste of Valrhona's Guanaja chocolate in this recipe (I also use it in the Guanaja Sherbet, page 32): That said, any good bittersweet chocolate would be fine.

| do-aheads |

*You can make the brownies and/or the frosting a day or two ahead and keep them in the refrigerator. Reheat the frosting in the microwave or over hot water to make it spreadable.

**The frosted brownies will keep, covered in the refrigerator, for up to 3 days.

| you'll need |

12 by 17-inch rimmed baking sheet

for the brownies

11 ounces Valrhona Guanaja chocolate, or other bittersweet chocolate

12 tablespoons (1 1/2 sticks) unsalted butter

1 1/3 cups sugar

3 large eggs, lightly beaten

3/4 cup all-purpose flour

1/4 cup cocoa powder

1/4 teaspoon salt

1 1/4 cups plus 2 to 3 tablespoons toasted and finely chopped walnuts

for the frosting

1 pound semi-sweet chocolate, finely chopped

2 cups heavy cream

2 teaspoons coffee liqueur

4 tablespoons (1/2 stick) unsalted butter, softened

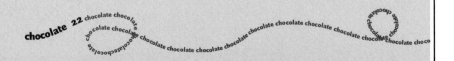

Position a rack in the lower third of the oven and preheat the oven to 375°F. Line a 12 by 17-inch rimmed baking sheet with foil and set aside.

For the brownies, in a mixing bowl set over (but not touching) a saucepan of hot water, melt the chocolate and butter. Remove the bowl from the heat and let cool slightly. Using a wooden spoon, stir in the sugar, eggs, flour, cocoa powder, salt, and 1¼ cups of the chopped walnuts (reserve the remaining chopped walnuts for decoration).

Spread the batter in the prepared pan. Bake for 10 minutes, then remove from the oven and set aside to cool. Put in the refrigerator to chill for at least 30 minutes before frosting.*

For the frosting, put the chocolate in a mixing bowl. In a saucepan, heat the cream just until it comes to a boil. Pour the cream over the chocolate and whisk until the chocolate melts. Whisk in the coffee liqueur and butter. Set aside for at least 20 minutes to cool and thicken slightly.*

Using a spatula, preferably an offset one, spread the frosting evenly over the brownie in the pan and then return to the refrigerator to chill again for about 30 minutes.**

Dipping a long sharp knife in hot water and drying it off each time, cut the brownies into 2-inch squares and then top with the remaining chopped walnuts. Let come to room temperature before serving.

black and white cream cheese
brownies

MAKES 16 BROWNIES

These classic dense and creamy chocolate and cream cheese brownies are good for children's lunch boxes, but adults love them, too.

| do-ahead |

*The cooled brownies can be covered and left in the pan at room temperature for up to 3 days. Cut them the same day you serve them.

| you'll need |

9-inch square baking pan

for the chocolate batter

3 tablespoons unsalted butter

4 ounces bittersweet chocolate

2 large eggs

3/4 cup sugar

1/2 cup all-purpose flour

1/2 teaspoon baking powder

1/2 teaspoon salt

1 teaspoon pure vanilla extract

for the cream cheese batter

2 tablespoons unsalted butter, softened

1 (3-ounce) package cream cheese, softened

1/4 cup sugar

1 large egg

1 tablespoon all-purpose flour

1 teaspoon pure vanilla extract

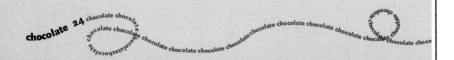

chocolate 24 chocolate chocolate chocolate chocolate chocolate chocolate chocolate chocolate chocolate chocolate chocolate chocolate chocolate chocolate choco

Preheat the oven to 350°F. Grease a 9-inch square baking pan and set it aside.

To make the chocolate batter, in a small saucepan melt the butter with the chocolate. In a bowl, whisk together the eggs and sugar. Stir in the flour, baking powder, salt, vanilla, and melted chocolate mixture until combined.

To make the cream cheese batter, in a mixer fitted with the paddle attachment, beat the butter and cream cheese until the mixture is light and fluffy. Stir in the sugar, egg, flour, and vanilla until well combined.

Pour half of the chocolate batter into the prepared pan, and then spread the cheesecake batter over that. Drop spoonfuls of the remaining chocolate batter on top. Drag a fork through the batter once or twice to create swirls.

Bake for 40 to 50 minutes or until the sides of the brownie pull away from the pan. Cool in the pan before cutting into 16 squares.*

deep chocolate **shortbread**

My own love of simple, pure flavors achieved with just a few ingredients began with my mom's love of butter suspended in time by flour, a little sugar, and salt—as in pie dough and shortbread. After making mounds of shortbread when I baked in England at a country-house hotel, I thought, "What can I do to make it different—better—next time?" As any chocoholic will tell you, what isn't better with chocolate? Here's a shortbread for chocolate lovers.

1 cup (2 sticks) unsalted butter, cut in $1/2$-inch pieces and softened

$3/4$ cup sugar

$1/2$ teaspoon pure vanilla extract

$13/4$ cups plus 2 tablespoons all-purpose flour

$1/2$ cup cocoa powder, preferably Dutch-processed

$1/4$ teaspoon salt

| do-aheads |

*You can make the dough up to 3 days in advance of baking: Shape it into a disk, wrap it well in plastic wrap, and store in the refrigerator. The dough can also be frozen for up to 2 months. Let the dough warm up on the counter for 30 minutes before rolling if it was refrigerated or at least an hour if frozen.

**Once the dough has been rolled out and put in the pan, it can be kept covered and refrigerated for up to 2 days before baking.

| you'll need |

Cookie sheet
Parchment paper

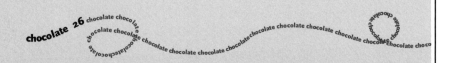

Line a cookie sheet with parchment and set aside.

In a mixer fitted with the paddle attachment, beat the butter and sugar until the mixture is pale and fluffy. Add the vanilla, flour, cocoa powder, and salt and mix until just blended.

Lightly dust a work surface with flour and turn the dough out onto it. Knead the dough by hand five to ten times, just enough to form it into a smooth ball.* Using a rolling pin, roll the dough out into a ¼-inch-thick square. Transfer the dough to the parchment-lined cookie sheet by rolling it up around the rolling pin and then unrolling it onto the paper. Roll the dough a little bit more once it's on the cookie sheet to make it slightly thinner (it's easier to transfer the dough when it's thicker). Using a fork (I like to entwine two forks to make it go more quickly), prick the surface of the dough all over to allow air to escape during baking. Put the pan in the refrigerator to chill for 30 minutes.**

Preheat the oven to 375°F.

Bake the shortbread until firm, 20 to 25 minutes. Remove the cookie sheet from the oven and immediately cut the shortbread into 24 rectangles. Let cool on the pan before storing in an airtight container at room temperature.

mocha **panna cotta**

At Tru, we serve this panna cotta in small demitasse cups — it's *that* rich and flavorful: bitter chocolate and coffee; sweet, salty caramel; and crunchy fleur de sel set against the smooth, tangy cream. If you don't have espresso cups, use any small container for these; think Japanese tea cups, egg cups, small ramekins, or even shot glasses. Fleur de sel, sea salt from the coast of France, is widely available in specialty markets or by mail order. You can use coarse sea salt or kosher salt, but although these other salts are still crunchy, you'll miss the unique flavor fleur de sel provides.

| do-aheads |

*The panna cotta can be made up to 2 days ahead and kept in the refrigerator.

**The caramel can be refrigerated for up to 1 week.

| you'll need |

12 small (2-ounce-capacity) containers

for the panna cotta

1 tablespoon water

1 1/4 teaspoons powdered gelatin

1 1/2 cups heavy cream

1/2 cup whole espresso beans

6 tablespoons sugar

2 1/2 ounces dark chocolate, chopped

1 cup sour cream

for the fleur de sel caramel

MAKES 3/4 CUP

3/4 cup sugar

1/4 cup water

1/2 cup heavy cream

1/4 teaspoon fleur de sel, or coarse sea salt or kosher salt, plus more for garnish

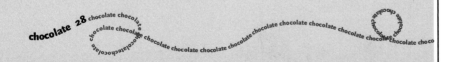

To make the panna cotta, put 1 tablespoon water in a small bowl and sprinkle the gelatin over the surface. Have ready 12 (2-ounce) demitasse cups or other small containers.

In a medium saucepan, combine the heavy cream, espresso beans, and sugar. Heat over medium-low heat until the mixture almost comes to a boil. Remove the pan from the heat and stir in the softened gelatin until it dissolves. Let the cream sit, off the heat, for 5 minutes to infuse it with the espresso flavor.

Put the chocolate in a bowl. Strain the hot espresso cream through a fine-mesh sieve over the chocolate and then whisk gently to melt the chocolate and combine. Whisk in the sour cream.

Pour the mixture into the cups. Chill in the refrigerator until the panna cotta is firm, at least 1 hour.*

To make the caramel, put the sugar in a high-sided medium saucepan. Spoon $\frac{1}{4}$ cup water down the inside walls of the pan and let it seep into the sugar to soak it, about 1 minute, drawing your finger in a cross through the middle of the sugar to help the water seep in, if needed. Heat the sugar over high heat until the sugar comes to a boil and then turns amber in color.

Immediately remove the pan from the heat and slowly pour in the cream, stirring gently but carefully with a wooden spoon: The mixture is extremely hot and will bubble up. Let the caramel cool before stirring in the fleur de sel.**

To serve, top the panna cotta with some of the caramel and sprinkle a little extra fleur de sel on top.

hot chocolate **pudding**

MAKES 3 TO 4 SERVINGS

A few years ago, my husband, Jimmy, and I traveled to the regal city of Saint Petersburg (Russia that is — not Florida) and were surprised to find the pastries not only so good but also so French. One thing that was neither familiar nor French, however, was a liquid hot chocolate pudding dispensed from a machine outfitted with a dasher (to prevent a skin from forming). It was served in espresso cups with a demitasse spoon holding a dollop of orange-scented whipped cream to stir into the cup and then to use to eat the pudding, tiny spoonful by tiny spoonful. I was enchanted by this wonderful late-night indulgence — and still am today.

To make the pudding, in a medium saucepan stir the sugar with the cornstarch, and then whisk in the milk, cream, and salt. Heat, whisking gently, over medium-high heat to just below the boiling point to thicken. Remove from the heat and stir in the vanilla, chocolate, and butter. Using a hand blender or a regular blender, whiz the mixture until it's very smooth.*

To make the whipped cream, combine the cream, sugar, and orange zest in a bowl and whip until soft peaks form.

To serve, pour the hot pudding into 3 to 4 espresso cups or 6-ounce ramekins and top with a dollop of whipped cream. Serve immediately.

| do-aheads |

*The pudding can be put into a container, covered with plastic wrap pressed lightly on the surface (to prevent a skin from forming), and refrigerated for up to 3 days. Reheat the pudding in a microwave or over simmering water on the stove for a few minutes, stirring several times, until hot.

**You can make the whipped cream up to 12 hours in advance and refrigerate it. Whip it again briefly before serving.

| you'll need |

Blender, preferably a hand blender

3 to 4 espresso cups or 6-ounce ceramic ramekins

for the pudding

1/2 cup sugar

1 1/2 tablespoons cornstarch

3/4 cup whole milk

1/2 cup heavy cream

Pinch of salt

1 teaspoon pure vanilla extract

9 ounces bittersweet chocolate, chopped

2 tablespoons (1/4 stick) unsalted butter

for the orange whipped cream

1/4 cup heavy cream

1 1/2 teaspoons granulated sugar

1/8 teaspoon grated orange zest

mexican hot chocolate **fondue**

MAKES 6 TO 8 SERVINGS

Similar to the beverage that goes back to the Maya and Aztecs, today's Mexican hot chocolate is made from bitter chocolate that has been mixed with coarse sugar and pressed into a disk that looks like a hockey puck. Hot water or milk is added to dissolve the chocolate and then it's spiked with roasted coffee and canela (a Mexican variety of cinnamon bark), a combination of flavors that's one of my favorites. I've used this hot chocolate as the inspiration for a silky dark chocolate fondue—still a fun way to serve dessert—accompanied by fruit, pound cake, and *real* marshmallows, which can often be found in upscale markets.

In a medium bowl, whisk together the sugar and cornstarch, and then slowly stir in the cream, milk, ground coffee, and canela. Pour the mixture into a large, heavy saucepan, add the vanilla bean, and bring to a boil slowly over medium heat. Simmer, whisking, for 4 minutes or until the mixture has thickened. Remove from the heat and whisk in the chocolate and butter until the butter has melted.

Strain through a fine-mesh sieve into a fondue pot set over a low flame and serve with the dippers and fondue forks.*

| do-ahead |

*The fondue can be made 2 days ahead, refrigerated, and gently reheated on top of the stove or in a microwave just until it's warm.

| you'll need |

Fondue pot with forks or wooden skewers

for the fondue

⅓ cup sugar

1 tablespoon cornstarch

1¼ cups heavy cream

1¼ cups whole milk

2 tablespoons ground coffee (medium grind)

½ teaspoon ground canela (Mexican cinnamon) or cinnamon

1 vanilla bean, halved lengthwise

7 ounces bittersweet chocolate, coarsely chopped

3 tablespoons unsalted butter

for the dippers

Good-quality or homemade marshmallows

Fresh fruit such as banana slices, strawberries, pear slices, or pineapple chunks

Pound cake, cut into chunks

guanaja **sherbet**

MAKES ABOUT 1 QUART, OR 8 SERVINGS

We serve this sherbet as part of Tru's "Chocolate Immersion" dessert, our most indulgent collection of chocolate with five different preparations offering an array of flavors and textures on one plate. Extravagant? Yes, but at home I wouldn't hesitate to serve this exotic, single-bean, velvety smooth, rich, chocolaty sherbet alone or together with White Chocolate Sherbet (page 75) or a store-bought cookie. This recipe is one of two recipes in this book—the other is the Best-Ever Fudgy Brownies on page 22)—in which I like to use Valrhona's Guanaja chocolate. It's worth seeking out for its nutty coffee-like flavor, but any good bittersweet chocolate will do.

Have ready near your cooktop a large bowl filled three-quarters full with ice and add enough water to cover the ice.

In a medium saucepan, bring 2½ cups water, the milk, brown sugar, corn syrup, cinnamon stick, and vanilla bean almost to a boil. Turn off the heat and whisk in the chocolate until it has melted. Strain through a fine-mesh sieve into a bowl and then place the bowl in the larger bowl of ice water. Stir occasionally until the mixture has chilled, about 10 minutes.*

Pour the sherbet mixture into the bowl of an ice cream maker and freeze according to the ice cream maker's instructions. Transfer to a container with a lid and freeze for at least 2 hours.**

| do-aheads |

*The sherbet base can be made 2 days ahead and refrigerated.

**The sherbet is best served the same day it's made, but can be kept frozen for 3 days. Let it soften slightly at room temperature for 10 minutes before serving if it seems too hard.

| you'll need |

Ice cream maker

2½ cups water

¾ cup whole milk

¾ cup brown sugar

¼ cup light corn syrup

1 cinnamon stick

1 vanilla bean, halved lengthwise

10½ ounces Valrhona Guanaja chocolate or other bittersweet chocolate, chopped

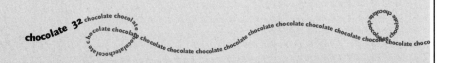

cocoa "cup" cakes

MAKES 12 SERVINGS

Here's a satisfying chocolate cake made from cocoa powder and baked in a mug. This is one place where quality counts. Buy the best Dutch-processed cocoa powder you can afford; you'll be glad you did when you taste the cakes' deep, rich, chocolaty flavor. To make them even more fun, top the "cup" cakes with marshmallows instead of whipped cream and run them under a broiler to give them a toasted marshmallow top.

Preheat the oven to 350°F. Place 12 heavy ceramic 8-ounce coffee cups or mugs 1½ inches apart on a 12 by 17-inch rimmed baking sheet or in a roasting pan.

To make the cakes, sift the sugar, flour, cocoa, baking powder, baking soda, and salt into the bowl of an electric mixer fitted with the whisk attachment. Blend the mixture briefly.

In a medium bowl, whisk the eggs, milk, oil, and vanilla until combined. Add to the dry ingredients in the mixer bowl and stir on low speed for 5 minutes. With the mixer on, gradually add the hot water, stirring until well blended. The batter will be quite thin.

Pour the batter into the coffee cups, filling them a little more than halfway, and bake until a skewer inserted in the center of the cakes comes out nearly clean (a few crumbs are okay) and the center feels firm to the touch, 25 to 30 minutes. Remove from the oven and let cool on the sheet.*

Whip the cream with the sugar until it holds a soft peak.**

To serve, spoon the whipped cream over the cup cakes.

do-aheads

*The cup cakes can be covered with plastic wrap and refrigerated for up to 4 days.

**The cream can be whipped up to 3 hours ahead of time, covered, and refrigerated until serving.

you'll need

12 heavy ceramic 8-ounce coffee cups or mugs

12 by 17-inch rimmed baking sheet or roasting pan

for the cake

3 cups sugar

2¾ cups all-purpose flour

1 cup plus 2 tablespoons cocoa powder, preferably Dutch-processed

2¼ teaspoons baking powder

2¼ teaspoons baking soda

1½ teaspoons salt

3 large eggs

1½ cups whole milk

¾ cup vegetable oil

1 tablespoon pure vanilla extract

1½ cups very hot water

for the whipped cream

1 cup heavy cream

1 tablespoon sugar

chocolate crêpes filled
with chocolate mousse

MAKES 6 SERVINGS

Crêpes and chocolate mousse, though slightly retro, have really never gone out of style. Though the recipe looks complicated and the finished dessert looks impressive on the plate, these are actually quite easy to make because all the components can be made ahead and then assembled at serving time.

| do-aheads |
*The crêpe batter can be made a day ahead and stored in the refrigerator. Just make sure you whisk it to recombine the flour before you begin cooking the crêpes.

**Store the stacked crêpes wrapped well in the freezer for up to 1 month. Defrost at room temperature before filling.

***The mousse should be made the day before you need it to give it time to set up properly.

| you'll need |
8- or 9-inch crêpe pan or nonstick sauté pan

for the crêpes
2 large eggs
½ cup plus 1 tablespoon whole milk
2 teaspoons granulated sugar
½ teaspoon salt
6 tablespoons all-purpose flour
2 tablespoons cocoa powder
2 tablespoons unsalted butter
Powdered sugar, for serving

for the chocolate mousse filling
4 ounces bittersweet chocolate, chopped
3 tablespoons granulated sugar
3 large egg yolks
1¼ cups heavy cream

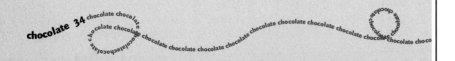

To make the crêpes, in a medium bowl, whisk the eggs well, and then whisk in the milk. Add the granulated sugar, salt, flour, and cocoa powder and whisk until combined. Let the mixture rest for 20 minutes in the refrigerator. Strain through a fine-mesh sieve.*

Heat an 8- or 9-inch crêpe pan or nonstick skillet over medium-high heat and add a little of the butter to coat the bottom of the pan. Pour or ladle 2 ounces of crêpe batter into the pan thinly and quickly swirl and tilt the pan so the batter spreads to cover the bottom of the pan evenly. Cook just until the surface of the batter begins to look dry, a minute or two, and then flip the crêpe over. Cook until the underside just begins to brown slightly, maybe 30 seconds, and then remove the crêpe to a plate or platter. Repeat with the remaining batter, buttering the pan between each crêpe and stacking them on the plate as they come out of the pan. You should have about 6 crepes.**

To make the chocolate mousse, put the chocolate in a medium heat-proof bowl and set the bowl over (but not touching) a saucepan of simmering water. Stir occasionally until the chocolate melts. Set the chocolate aside to cool slightly; reserve the pan of water.

Combine the granulated sugar, egg yolks, and 1/4 cup of the cream in another heat-proof bowl and whisk well to combine. Set the bowl over (but not touching) the saucepan of simmering water. Whisk continuously until the mixture thickens and leaves trails from the whisk, about 5 minutes. Remove the bowl from the saucepan and set aside off the heat.

Whip the remaining 1 cup cream until it holds a soft peak.

Whisk half of the whipped cream into the melted chocolate and then, using a rubber spatula, fold in the egg-yolk mixture. Fold in the remaining whipped cream and chill in the refrigerator until you're ready to fill and serve the crêpes.***

To serve, cut the crepes in half into half-moons. Place a scoop of mousse in the center of each crêpe half and fold the points of the crêpe over to form a cone shape around the mousse. Place 2 crêpe cones in each of 6 shallow serving bowls and dust with powdered sugar.

chocolate **babka**

My family (and a few others for that matter) never had to make this old-world yeasted sweet bread at home because there are so many great neighborhood Polish and Russian bakeries in Chicago. I learned the recipe from Lydia, the Austrian breakfast chef at a restaurant where I worked in Rochester, New York. I used to show up at work two hours before my 8:00 a.m. shift, just to bake with her in the morning when the chef wasn't around to see us making babka. Making a sponge helps jump-start the yeast for its long journey up ahead. This all-day project will make your home smell like heaven.

| do-aheads |

*The filling can be made up to 2 days ahead and stored in the refrigerator.

**The pan can be covered with plastic wrap and kept in the refrigerator overnight. Let the dough sit at room temperature for 30 minutes or until it has doubled in volume before baking.

| you'll need |

9-inch round cake pan

for the sponge

½ cup all-purpose flour

1½ teaspoons sugar

1½ ounces cake (fresh) yeast or 1 generous tablespoon active dry yeast

1 cup warm milk (about 95°F)

for the dough

1 large egg

5 large egg yolks

½ cup plus 2 tablespoons sugar

½ teaspoon salt

⅛ teaspoon pure vanilla extract

1½ cups all-purpose flour

4 tablespoons (½ stick) unsalted butter, melted

for the chocolate filling

1 (7-ounce) tube almond paste

1 large egg white

1 tablespoon unsalted butter, softened

4 ounces bittersweet chocolate, chopped

 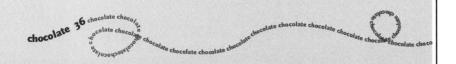

Make the sponge by stirring together the flour, sugar, yeast, and warm milk in a medium bowl. Cover the bowl with plastic wrap and let sit at room temperature for 1 hour, until bubbly.

To make the dough, in the bowl of an electric mixer fitted with the paddle, stir the egg, egg yolks, sugar, salt, and vanilla until well blended. Add the flour and sponge and blend with a dough hook until combined. Drizzle in the melted butter. Mix for a minute or so longer, until a shaggy dough forms.

Turn the dough out onto a lightly floured work surface. Knead the dough for 3 to 5 minutes, until it's smooth and elastic but not sticky. Lightly grease a large bowl, put the dough in the bowl, and cover with plastic wrap. Let rise at room temperature until doubled in volume, about 1½ hours.

Meanwhile make the filling: In a mixer or food processor, blend the almond paste, egg white, and butter until smooth. Add the chocolate and mix until just combined. Set aside.*

Turn the dough out onto a lightly floured work surface and punch it down until it's deflated. Using a rolling pin, roll the dough into an 8 by 14-inch rectangle that's about ¼-inch thick and let rest for 5 minutes covered with a tea towel to keep it from drying out.

Spread the filling over the dough to within ½ inch of the edges, and then roll up the dough lengthwise, jelly-roll style, pinching the seam along the bottom of the roll together to seal it. Flatten the dough slightly with the rolling pin and then, holding down the dough on one end, twist the other end 6 to 8 times.

Place one end of the log of dough at the center of a 9-inch cake pan and then wrap the log around itself to form a spiral (snail shell shape) in the pan.** Cover the pan lightly with a clean, damp kitchen towel, and let rise until doubled in volume, about 30 minutes to 1 hour.

Preheat the oven to 350°F.

Bake the babka until it's golden brown, about 45 minutes. Remove from the pan and let cool on a rack.

chocolate-almond
upside-down cake

MAKES ONE 10-INCH CAKE, OR 10 SERVINGS

Who says upside-down cake has to be a vanilla cake with pineapple rings and maraschino cherries? This chocolate cake with a gooey-nutty topping is an upside-down cake designed for chocolate lovers. I like it made with almonds, but you can use whatever kind of nuts you like best, say hazelnuts or walnuts, or combine several kinds to clean out the pantry. If there happens to be any cake left over you'll find it's great the next day. Note that a serrated knife cuts the cake more easily than a regular blade.

| do-ahead |
*The cake keeps at room temperature for up to 2 days.

| you'll need |
10-inch round cake pan

for the caramel topping

6 tablespoons ($^3/_4$ stick) unsalted butter, melted

$^3/_4$ cup packed light brown sugar

$^1/_4$ cup honey

$1^1/_4$ cups sliced or slivered almonds, lightly toasted

for the cake

$1^1/_4$ cups cake flour

$^1/_2$ cup cocoa powder, preferably Dutch-processed

1 teaspoon baking soda

$^1/_2$ teaspoon salt

8 tablespoons (1 stick) unsalted butter, softened

$1^1/_2$ cups sugar

3 large eggs

1 cup buttermilk

1 teaspoon pure vanilla extract

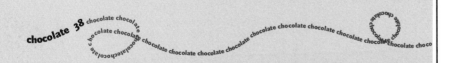

Generously grease a 10-inch round cake pan. To make the topping, pour the melted butter into the cake pan and swirl to coat the bottom; then sprinkle in the brown sugar. Drizzle in the honey and sprinkle the almonds evenly over the bottom.

Preheat the oven to 350°F.

To make the cake batter, sift the flour, cocoa powder, baking soda, and salt together three times (this is to make the cake extra light). Beat the butter in a mixer fitted with a whisk attachment until smooth and fluffy. Add the sugar and mix. One at a time, add the eggs, mixing after each addition. Beat until fluffy and light, about 3 minutes. With the mixer running on low speed, add a third of the dry ingredients and mix to combine. Mix in half of the buttermilk, and then another third of the dry ingredients, before adding the remaining buttermilk and the vanilla. Finish with the remaining dry ingredients and mix until smooth. Pour the batter into the pan.

Bake until set in the center and springy, 25 to 35 minutes. Run a knife around the edge of the pan and immediately invert the pan onto a serving platter. Let it sit with the pan still on top for 5 minutes so the caramel can soak into the cake a bit, before removing the pan. If the topping is sticking to the pan, warm the pan surface over a low burner to loosen the caramel and then pour it over the cake. Let cool completely.* Cut into wedges with a serrated knife.

chocolate-praline **cake in a jar**

For a few years now I've been a judge at the Whirlpool Accubake Unique Cake Contest, which is similar to the Pillsbury Bake-Off. A chocolate cake with a pecan and butterscotch toffee topping called Chocolate Coffee Toffee Cake by Elizabeth Kisch from Pennsylvania won first place in 2002 and the $10,000 prize, which she donated to Heifer International. Elizabeth told me she made her cakes in glass canning jars and would tuck one into her husband's business trip luggage so he wouldn't miss his favorite cake while he was out of town. This simplified version of her cake would be perfect to take to a picnic or even a backyard barbecue.

| do-aheads |

*The cakes can be made ahead, cooled, covered, and kept at room temperature for 2 days or in the refrigerator for up to 4 days.

**The finished cakes will keep for up to 4 days at room temperature.

| you'll need |

Ten to twelve 1-pint glass canning jars

Rimmed baking sheet or roasting pan

for the cake

8 tablespoons (1 stick) unsalted butter, softened

1 1/2 cups packed light brown sugar

2 large eggs

1 teaspoon pure vanilla extract

6 tablespoons unsweetened cocoa powder

1 1/2 teaspoons baking soda

1/4 teaspoon salt

1 1/2 cups sifted cake flour

2/3 cup sour cream

2/3 cup brewed coffee (I just use the morning's leftover coffee)

for the praline topping

2 tablespoons unsalted butter

3/4 cup firmly packed light brown sugar

1/2 cup water

1 cup powdered sugar

1/2 cup pecan halves or pieces

Preheat the oven to 350°F. Place 10 to 12 1-pint glass canning jars on a rimmed baking sheet, evenly arranged with space between them. (If you have a Silpat liner, place it under the jars to prevent them from sliding around.)

To make the cakes, in a mixer fitted with a whisk attachment, beat the butter until smooth. Add the brown sugar and eggs and mix until fluffy, about 2 minutes. Add the vanilla, cocoa, baking soda, and salt and mix until combined. Add half of the flour, then half of the sour cream, and mix until combined. Repeat with the remaining flour and sour cream. Drizzle in the coffee and mix until smooth. The batter will be thin, like heavy cream.

Pour the batter into the jars, filling them halfway. Bake until the tops of the cakes are firm to the touch, about 25 minutes.*

To make the topping, melt the butter in a medium saucepan over medium heat, then add the brown sugar and 1/2 cup water and stir with a wooden spoon until the sugar is dissolved, 2 to 3 minutes. Remove the pan from the heat and stir in the powdered sugar until combined, then return to the heat and bring to a boil. Stir in the nuts.

Pour the praline topping over the cakes to cover, working quickly, because the praline hardens quickly as it cools. Let the cakes cool completely if they aren't already, before screwing on jar lids.**

chocolate fudge **soccer cakes**

A couple of years ago someone gave me a pan with individual lozenge-shaped molds for making homemade Twinkie-style cakes. The 8-slot cake pans are still available (see Sources, page 79), but if you don't have one, you can use a rectangular cake pan and then cut the cake into smaller rectangles. Bucking tradition, I go for chocolate cake and vanilla "frosting" filling in this recipe instead of yellow sponge cake and cream filling. I make this with my son, Gio, when he needs to take the snack for soccer; the cake is great for anyone who has a milk allergy (like one of Gio's friends, Eric Guberman) because it's made without milk or butter.

| do-aheads |

*The cakes (or single uncut cake) can be stored in an airtight container overnight or wrapped in plastic and refrigerated for up to 3 days.

**The filling can be made 2 days ahead and kept covered in the refrigerator. Bring it to room temperature before piping it into the cakes.

***The cakes are still delicious after 2 days if kept covered at room temperature.

| you'll need |

2 pans of individual lozenge-shaped cake molds or one 9 by-13-inch cake pan

Drinking straw

Pastry bag with a medium (1/4-inch) plain tip

for the chocolate cake

3 cups all-purpose flour

2 cups granulated sugar

1/2 cup cocoa powder

2 teaspoons baking soda

1 teaspoon salt

2/3 cup vegetable oil

2 teaspoons white vinegar

1 teaspoon pure vanilla extract

2 cups cold water

for the vanilla filling

14 tablespoons (1¾ sticks) unsalted butter, softened

1½ cups powdered sugar, plus more if needed

1/2 to 1 tablespoon milk

1/8 teaspoon pure vanilla extract

 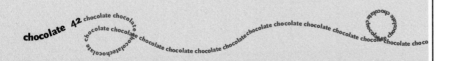

Preheat the oven to 350°F. Have ready 2 pans of greased oval sponge cake molds or a parchment-lined 9 by 13-inch baking pan.

To make the cakes, in a large bowl, whisk together the flour, granulated sugar, cocoa, baking soda, and salt. Add the oil, vinegar, vanilla, and cold water and stir with a whisk for 1 minute, or until combined. Divide the batter equally among the molds of the pans, filling them halfway, or pour into the baking pan. Bake until the cake springs back when touched in the center, 20 to 25 minutes for individual cakes or 30 to 35 minutes for the large cake. If using the molds, turn the cakes out of the pan right away while they're still hot. For a large cake, let the cake cool in the pan for 20 to 30 minutes. Invert onto a rack and let cool completely.*

To make the filling, in a mixer, beat the butter until light and fluffy, about 5 minutes. Add the powdered sugar, $\frac{1}{2}$ tablespoon milk, and the vanilla and beat until smooth. Add additional milk or powdered sugar until you get a consistency that can be piped.**

If you used a 9 by 13-inch pan, chill the cake in the refrigerator for 1 hour to make it easier to cut and fill. Remove the parchment and cut the cake in half lengthwise, and then crosswise into fingers that are as wide as the cake is high. (For example if your cake is $1\frac{1}{2}$ inches high, the fingers should be $1\frac{1}{2}$ inches wide.) This should give you 16 small cakes.

Push a drinking straw through the middle of the cakes the long way to create a channel. Place the filling in a pastry bag fitted with a medium ($\frac{1}{4}$-inch) plain tip and pipe the filling into each end of the cakes to fill them completely, watching that the center expands slightly to assure the filling has gone all the way to the center.***

cream cheese–stuffed
chocolate cupcakes

MAKES 2 DOZEN CUPCAKES

These moist and rich chocolate cupcakes have a heart of sweet cream cheese, a yummy and satisfying surprise. Vinegar keeps the cake tender because it inhibits gluten from developing when beating the flour in the batter. These are always a hit at my son Gio's school bake sale, but they're definitely worth more than the mandatory price of a quarter, if you ask me!

| do-aheads |

*The cupcakes can be baked up to 2 weeks ahead and frozen in an airtight container or resealable bag.

**The frosting can be made up to 1 week in advance, covered, and refrigerated. Let sit at room temperature for an hour or so to warm up to a spreadable consistency.

***The frosted cupcakes will keep for 3 days at room temperature.

| you'll need |

Two 12-cup muffin tins

Cupcake paper liners

for the filling

4 ounces cream cheese, softened

1 large egg yolk

1 teaspoon pure vanilla extract

$1/3$ cup sugar

$2/3$ cup semi-sweet chocolate chips

for the cupcakes

3 cups all-purpose flour

2 cups sugar

$1/2$ cup cocoa powder, preferably Dutch-processed

2 teaspoons baking soda

1 teaspoon salt

2 cups hot water

$3/4$ cup vegetable oil

2 teaspoons white vinegar

1 tablespoon instant coffee crystals (optional)

1 tablespoon pure vanilla extract

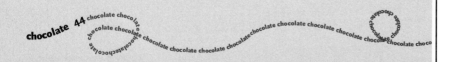

To make the filling, in a mixer fitted with a paddle attachment, beat the cream cheese until fluffy, about 5 minutes, scraping the bowl often, and then blend in the egg yolk and vanilla. Add the sugar and chips and mix for a few seconds on low to fold them in.

Preheat the oven to 350°F. Line 2 muffin tins with cupcake paper liners.

To make the cupcakes, in a large bowl, whisk together the flour, sugar, cocoa, baking soda, and salt. In a large measuring cup, combine the water, oil, vinegar, instant coffee, and vanilla. Pour the mixture into the dry ingredients and whisk until just combined (don't worry if there are a few lumps).

Fill each cupcake liner two-thirds full of batter. Drop a heaping teaspoon of the cream cheese filling into the center of each.

Bake for 30 to 35 minutes, or until the cupcakes have puffed on top and are firm to the touch. Remove from the oven and let cool completely in the tins.*

continued on page 46

for the chocolate frosting

8 tablespoons unsalted butter

$1\frac{1}{2}$ cups superfine sugar

$1\frac{1}{2}$ cups cocoa powder, preferably
  Dutch-processed

Pinch of salt

1 cup heavy cream

1 teaspoon instant coffee crystals
  (optional)

$\frac{1}{2}$ cup sour cream

$1\frac{1}{2}$ teaspoons pure vanilla extract

To make the frosting, melt the butter in a large saucepan. Stir in the superfine sugar, cocoa, and salt. The mixture might look grainy or sandy and this is fine. Whisk the cream and instant coffee into the cocoa mixture and cook over low heat, while stirring to dissolve the sugar grains. The mixture should get hot to the touch but never simmer or boil. Remove from the heat and stir in the sour cream and vanilla. Let cool until the frosting thickens and becomes spreadable, about 1 hour. If it seems too thin, stir in some powdered sugar.**

Remove the cupcakes from the tins. Spread the frosting on the tops of the cupcakes.***

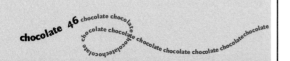

heart throbs with
marshmallow filling

MAKES ABOUT 12 INDIVIDUAL CAKES,
DEPENDING ON THE SIZE OF YOUR COOKIE CUTTER

I love it when I have an opportunity to make treats for my son's class parties. One year for Valentine's Day I was particularly inspired. I made these small sandwiches of chocolate heart-shaped cakes and my son, Gio, got to pipe the marshmallow filling on without any help from me. Gio specifically wants me to suggest this recipe next time you want to cook with your kids.

Preheat the oven to 350°F. Grease a 12 by 17-inch rimmed baking sheet or jelly-roll pan and line the bottom with parchment or wax paper.

To make the cake, combine the sugar, flour, cocoa, baking powder, baking soda, and salt in the bowl of an electric mixer fitted with the whisk attachment. Mix just until combined. In a medium bowl, whisk the eggs with the milk, oil, and vanilla. Add to the dry ingredients and mix on low speed for 5 minutes. Gradually add the hot water just until combined. The batter will be quite thin.

continued on page 48

| do-aheads |

*You can make the cake ahead, wrap it well, and freeze it for up to a month.

**The assembled cakes can be kept for 2 to 3 days at room temperature if well wrapped.

| you'll need |

12 by 17-inch rimmed baking sheet or jelly-roll pan

Parchment paper or wax paper

Candy thermometer

Heart-shaped cookie cutter (approximately 2½ by 2½ inches)

Pastry bag and large (½-inch) plain tip

for the cake

3 cups sugar

2¾ cups all-purpose flour

1 cup plus 2 tablespoons cocoa powder, preferably Dutch-processed

2¼ teaspoons baking powder

2¼ teaspoons baking soda

1½ teaspoons salt

3 large eggs

1¼ cups whole milk

¾ cup vegetable oil

1 tablespoon pure vanilla extract

1¼ cups very hot water

Pour the batter into the prepared pan. Bake until a skewer inserted in the center of the cake comes out clean (a few crumbs are okay) and the center feels firm to the touch, 25 to 30 minutes. Let the cake cool in the pan. Cover with plastic wrap and chill in the refrigerator or freezer for at least an hour until you're ready to cut the cake; the cakes are most easily cut after they have been frozen.*

To make the marshmallow filling, put the 2 tablespoons cold water in a small bowl and gradually sprinkle the gelatin over the top. Set aside to soften.

Combine the sugar, corn syrup, and the remaining $\frac{1}{4}$ cup water in a medium saucepan fitted with a candy thermometer. Bring the mixture to a boil and cook to the softball stage, about 235°F.

Meanwhile, in a clean electric mixer bowl fitted with a clean whisk attachment, whip the egg whites on medium-high speed until they hold soft peaks and then turn the mixer to the lowest speed.

As soon as the syrup mixture reaches 235°F, remove the pan from the heat, add the gelatin mixture, and swirl the pan to mix it in.

With the mixer on medium speed, slowly pour the syrup in a slow stream over the whites and continue to whip until the whites hold stiff peaks, 3 to 5 minutes. Mix in the

for the marshmallow filling

2 tablespoons plus $\frac{1}{4}$ cup cold water
1 tablespoon powdered gelatin
$\frac{3}{4}$ cup sugar
$\frac{1}{4}$ cup light corn syrup
2 large egg whites
$\frac{1}{4}$ teaspoon pure vanilla extract
A few drops red food coloring
Red sugar, for sprinkling

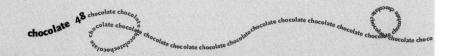

vanilla and red food coloring to turn the mixture pink. Set aside but don't let it cool completely; you want to be able to pipe it before it sets up.

While the whites are beating, use a heart-shaped cookie cutter (mine is about $2\frac{1}{2}$ inches wide, but use what you have to make larger or smaller cakes) to cut out heart-shaped cakes; place them on a cookie sheet.

To fill and assemble the cakes, use a pastry bag with a large ($\frac{1}{2}$-inch) plain tip to pipe the marshmallow filling on half the cake hearts to cover the surface. Top with the remaining cake hearts to form sandwiches (if you wound up with an odd number of cakes, you'll have one left for the chef). Pipe a heart on top of each cake: Pipe 2 upside-down teardrops in a "V," meeting at the bottom to form each heart. Sprinkle the marshmallow on top lightly with red sugar.**

mini **chocolate chip muffins**

MAKES 2 DOZEN MINI MUFFINS

Usually I'm a stickler about not using substitutes for butter, but peanut butter lends a wonderful richness to this recipe. My son, Gio, and his friends love these tiny muffins packed with chocolate chips, but whenever you serve them, particularly at school events, make sure no one is allergic to peanuts. Most people will not suspect the "secret" ingredient.

Preheat the oven to 375°F. Line 2 mini muffin tins with paper liners.

In a mixer fitted with the whisk attachment, mix the peanut butter, egg, and granulated and brown sugars until smooth. Add the milk in thirds, mixing well after each addition.

In a medium bowl, stir together the flour, baking powder, and salt. Add the dry ingredients to the peanut-butter mixture. Combine on low speed just until the flour streaks disappear. Stir in the chocolate chips.

Spoon the batter into the muffin cups, filling them three quarters of the way to the top. Bake the muffins for 10 to 15 minutes, or until the muffins have puffed and are firm on top. Remove from the oven and let cool in the tins.*

| do-ahead |

*Put the muffins in a resealable plastic bag and freeze them for up to 2 months. Let them thaw at room temperature before serving.

| you'll need |

2 mini muffin tins with 12 molds each
24 mini muffin paper liners

1 cup chunky peanut butter
1 large egg
1/3 cup granulated sugar
1/3 cup packed light brown sugar
1 cup whole milk
1 1/2 cups all-purpose flour
1 tablespoon baking powder
1/4 teaspoon salt
1/2 cup mini semi-sweet chocolate chips

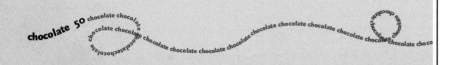

chocolate 50 chocolate chocolate chocolate chocolate chocolate chocolate chocolate chocolate chocolate chocolate chocolate chocolate chocolate chocolate chocolate chocolate choco

chocolate waffles with
banana ganache

MAKES 4 SERVINGS

It's hard to decide whether it's the crisp-on-the-outside chocolate waffle or the yummy banana ganache that brings out the kid in me. I do know that both children and grown-ups adore these waffles, whether they're served for dessert or an indulgent breakfast.

Preheat a waffle iron.

To make the waffles, in a mixer fitted with the whisk attachment, whip the egg whites on high speed, until they hold soft peaks, then add the sugar and continue whipping until the whites are stiff but not dry.

In a large mixing bowl, whisk together the yolks and milk. Add the flour, cocoa powder, baking powder, and butter and mix until smooth. Switch to a rubber spatula and fold in the whipped egg whites.

Cook the waffles according to the manufacturer's instructions. Set aside.*

To make the banana ganache, put the chocolate in a heat-proof bowl set over (but not touching) a saucepan of simmering water and stir occasionally until melted. Remove from the heat. Whisk in the cream, corn syrup, and banana. Cover and refrigerate for at least 6 hours.**

To serve, break the waffles into sections. Place 2 waffle sections on each of 4 dessert plates. Top with a spoonful of banana ganache and some ice cream.

| do-aheads |

*Waffles can be made 1 day in advance, covered, and stored at room temperature.

**The banana ganache will keep for up to 3 days in the refrigerator.

| you'll need |

Waffle iron, preferably with 4 small waffle sections

for the waffles

2 large eggs, separated

2 tablespoons sugar

1$\frac{1}{2}$ cups milk

1 cup all-purpose flour

2 tablespoons cocoa powder, preferably Dutch-processed

2 teaspoons baking powder

8 tablespoons (1 stick) unsalted butter, melted

for the banana ganache

8 ounces semi-sweet chocolate

$\frac{1}{4}$ cup heavy cream

1 tablespoon light corn syrup

1 very ripe banana, mashed

1 pint vanilla ice cream, frozen yogurt, or vanilla yogurt

peanut butter and chocolate
chip **thumbprints**

MAKES 30 COOKIES

One of my best girlfriends, Karen Katz, introduced me to these delicious cookies studded with chocolate chips and filled with a fudgy chocolate pool. I take the recipe a step farther by adding peanut butter, having been inspired by Reese's Peanut Butter Cups. I made them for Christmas one year to take to my husband's family in Delaware, so I know they travel well, freeze well, and get eaten fast, with a glass of cold milk, of course.

| do-aheads |

*The unfilled cookies can be kept at room temperature for 1 day or frozen for up to 1 month.

**The filling can be made 1 week ahead, covered, and refrigerated, but it must be warmed before filling the cookies.

***Filled cookies will keep in an airtight container for 5 days.

| you'll need |

Cookie sheet

A thumb!

for the cookies

8 tablespoons (1 stick) unsalted butter, softened

1/2 cup packed light brown sugar

1 teaspoon pure vanilla extract

1 1/2 cups all-purpose flour

1/2 teaspoon salt

2 tablespoons milk

1/4 cup semi-sweet chocolate chips, chopped

1/4 cup chopped roasted salted peanuts

for the filling

3/4 cup semi-sweet chocolate chips

2 tablespoons peanut butter

2 tablespoons corn syrup

1 tablespoon water

1 teaspoon pure vanilla extract

Preheat the oven to 375°F.

To make the cookies, in a mixer fitted with the paddle attachment, beat the butter until light and fluffy, about 3 minutes. Add the brown sugar and vanilla and mix on medium-low speed. Mix in the flour and salt, then add the milk and chocolate chips and mix until combined.

Using your hands, roll pieces of dough into 1½-inch balls and dip the top of the balls in the chopped peanuts. Place peanut-side up 1½ inches apart on a cookie sheet. Push your thumb into the middle of each cookie to make a deep impression.

Bake the cookies for 10 to 12 minutes, or until they're light golden brown. Let cool on the cookie sheet while you make the filling.*

To make the filling, melt the chocolate chips in a medium bowl set over (but not touching) a saucepan of simmering water. Stir in the peanut butter, corn syrup, 1 tablespoon water, and the vanilla until combined.** Let cool for 5 minutes. Using a spoon, fill the centers of the cookies with the filling. Let sit for 30 minutes to set.***

chocolate **madeleines**

MAKES 2 DOZEN MADELEINES

I've been entrusted with many kitchen heirlooms, including my great-grandmother's rolling pin and my grandmother's ginger jar, which I treasure, but I was brought to tears when I realized the honor and responsibility that was placed in my hands when I inherited Julia Child's madeleine molds. From the well-seasoned appearance of the molds it's obvious that she must have made many batches of the golden, buttery little shell-shaped cakes immortalized by Proust, but I don't think Julia, trailblazer that she was, would mind that I use her molds to make this seductive chocolate version. Skip Proust's herbal tea and dip these into coffee, black tea with milk, or, of course, hot chocolate, if desired.

| do-ahead |

*The batter can be covered and refrigerated for up to 4 days or frozen for 2 weeks. Sometimes I even freeze it right in the pastry bag with no tip, keeping the ends shut with rubberbands.

| you'll need |

2 madeleine molds
Pastry bag with a large (½-inch) plain tip (optional)

- 8 tablespoons (1 stick) unsalted butter, plus 4 tablespoons, softened for buttering the madeleine molds
- 3 large eggs
- ½ cup granulated sugar
- 2 tablespoons packed dark brown sugar
- 1 cup cake flour
- ¼ cup cocoa powder, preferably Dutch-processed
- 1½ teaspoons baking powder
- ⅛ teaspoon salt
- ¼ teaspoon pure vanilla extract

 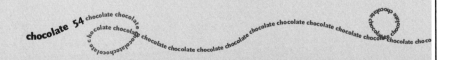

Preheat the oven to 325°F. Brush the madeleine pans well with the 4 tablespoons softened butter and put in the refrigerator for 5 minutes (to harden the butter and keep it in place).

In a small, heavy saucepan, melt the remaining 8 tablespoons butter over medium heat. Continue to cook until the butter turns golden brown, being careful not to let the butter burn. Remove from the heat, strain through a fine-mesh sieve into a small bowl, and set aside.

In a mixer fitted with the whisk attachment, whip the eggs with the granulated and brown sugars until the mixture is light and thickened, 3 to 5 minutes. Add the cake flour, cocoa powder, baking powder, and salt, and stir on low speed until combined. Add the vanilla and browned butter and mix just until blended.*

Insert a large (½-inch) plain tip into a pastry bag and fill it with the batter. Pipe mounds of batter into the prepared pans to fill the molds, mounding the batter in the center of the molds but not filling to the edge. Alternatively, you can use a teaspoon to fill the molds with batter. Bake for 8 to 10 minutes, or until the madeleines are firm and a little mound is puffed up in the middle. Once baked, the madeleines are best eaten the same day.

creamy dreamy **walnut fudge**

MAKES 80 PIECES

I once spent a whole week of my life just making fudge. It was for a fudge cart at a restaurant Oprah Winfrey was opening in Chicago. I made peanut butter fudge, marshmallow fudge, maple fudge, you name it. I got pretty good at it if I do say so myself. Agitating or mixing the chocolate mixture as it cools helps to create tiny sugar crystals that make the fudge silky smooth as it dissolves on your tongue.

Grease a 9-inch square baking pan and set aside.

In a medium saucepan, stir the chocolate and milk over low heat until the chocolate is melted. Add the sugar, corn syrup, and salt, hook a candy thermometer onto the pot, and cook the mixture to the soft-ball stage (235°F). Add the butter, then scrape the mixture into the bowl of a mixer fitted with the paddle attachment.

Beat on medium speed until the mixture begins to lighten in color, 3 to 6 minutes, adding the vanilla in the first minute. Add the nuts and continue beating on low speed until the fudge loses its gloss and thickens, 2 to 3 minutes.

Pour into the prepared pan, spreading it out evenly, preferably with an offset spatula. Let cool completely before cutting into 1-inch squares.*

| do-ahead |

*The fudge keeps in an airtight container for at least 2 weeks.

| you'll need |

Candy thermometer
9-inch square baking pan

4 ounces unsweetened chocolate, chopped

1¼ cups milk

3 cups sugar

2 tablespoons light corn syrup

⅛ teaspoon salt

4 tablespoons (½ stick) unsalted butter

1 teaspoon pure vanilla extract

½ cup chopped walnuts, toasted (optional)

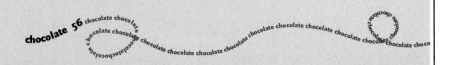

hot fudge **sundaes**

MAKES 4 TO 6 SERVINGS

In the 1960s my dad and my brother, Gary, and I used to play folk music at a coffeehouse in Highwood, Illinois. I was maybe six or seven years old at the time and we used to look forward to our compensation for singing and playing: a huge hot fudge sundae after each performance. Many years later when I was the pastry chef at the Pump Room in Chicago we made a diminutive version called "The World's Smallest Hot Fudge Sundae," and the dessert was so popular that I had to make a five-gallon bucket of the sauce every other day! Needless to say, this chewy chocolate sauce doubles and triples well, so make some to jar up for friends, too.

To make the hot fudge sauce, combine the heavy cream, chocolate, sugar, corn syrup, and butter in a large saucepan and bring to a boil over medium-high heat. Turn down the heat so that the mixture barely simmers, and cook until it appears to be separating, 30 to 60 minutes. Although this seems like a big time range, the amount of time it takes for the separation to happen depends on the chocolate and the butterfat content of the cream; the breaking is what you're looking for.

Remove the pan from the heat and whisk in the vanilla. Using an immersion blender (or a regular stand blender), process the sauce for 1 minute to smooth it out.*

To assemble the sundaes, whip the cream with the sugar until the cream holds soft peaks.

Serve spoonfuls of the hot fudge sauce over vanilla ice cream and top with the whipped cream and peanuts.

| **do-ahead** |

*The sauce keeps well in the fridge for up to 3 weeks. Warm the sauce in the top of a double boiler or in a microwave before serving.

| **you'll need** |

Immersion blender or regular blender

for the hot fudge sauce

3 cups heavy cream

4 ounces unsweetened chocolate, broken into pieces

1 cup sugar

1/4 cup light corn syrup

4 tablespoons (1/2 stick) unsalted butter

1 tablespoon pure vanilla extract

for the sundaes

1 cup heavy cream

2 tablespoons sugar

1 pint vanilla ice cream

Chopped roasted, salted peanuts (preferably Spanish)

chocolate-dipped

peanut butter balls

MAKES 3 DOZEN BALLS

I love regular peanut butter balls, but these little gems are made even better with the crunch of crisp puffed rice, and then enrobed in a thin coating of melted milk and semi-sweet chocolates. They make a great after-school snack or after-dinner treat.

In an electric mixer fitted with the paddle, or by hand, mix the powdered sugar, peanut butter, and butter on low speed until well combined. Mix in the puffed rice cereal.

Using your hands, form the mixture into walnut-size balls (about 1 generous tablespoon each) and refrigerate until firm, about 1 hour.*

Stir the chocolates together in a heat-proof bowl and set the bowl over (but not touching) a saucepan of simmering water. Stir occasionally until the chocolates are melted and smooth. Stir in the vegetable oil.

Using a fork, dip the peanut butter balls into the melted chocolate, rolling them around so they are entirely coated, then fish them out with a fork, shake them off a bit, and set the coated balls on a parchment-lined cookie sheet. Set aside for at least 2 hours to cool and set up.**

| do aheads |

*The peanut butter balls can be kept in the refrigerator for up to 4 days before dipping in chocolate.

**The peanut butter balls can sit for as long as 8 hours at room temperature before serving. They will keep in an air-tight container in the refrigerator for up to 2 weeks.

| you'll need |

Cookie sheet
Parchment or wax paper

4$\frac{1}{4}$ cups powdered sugar

2 cups creamy peanut butter

8 tablespoons (1 stick) unsalted butter, softened

3 cups crisp puffed rice cereal

12 ounces semi-sweet chocolate, chopped

12 ounces milk chocolate, chopped

2 tablespoons vegetable oil

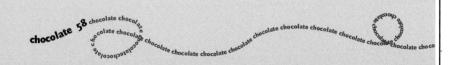

peanut butter

cocoa crisp treats

MAKES 3 DOZEN PIECES

I made up this recipe for a kids' cooking class I taught about making healthier after-school snacks using rice. The classes were organized by a charitable foundation called Common Threads (founded by Art Smith, Oprah Winfrey's chef; I'm on their advisory board), which teaches children about racial and ethnic diversity through cooking different ethnic recipes. This recipe brings together the crunchy chocolate cereal with peanut butter for added energy and protein. As a final touch the treats are drizzled with a little more chocolate, for extra flavor and fun.

Put the puffed rice cereal in a bowl. Have ready 3 nonstick mini muffin tins or a greased 9 by 13-inch baking dish or pan.

In a saucepan, stir together the brown sugar and corn syrup. Bring to a boil over high heat and boil for 1 minute. Turn off the heat and stir in the peanut butter until combined.

Immediately pour the hot syrup over the rice cereal and quickly stir until thoroughly combined.

Using your hands, while the mixture is still warm, press it into the mini muffin tins or baking dish. Let cool for at least 15 minutes, or until firm and set. Unmold from the tins or baking dish.*

Using a spoon, drizzle lines of the melted chocolate over the top of the cooled treats. If you used a baking dish, cut into bars before serving.**

| do-aheads |

*Drizzle with chocolate the day you serve them if you like.

**Stored in an airtight tin, these can be kept at room temperature for up to 1 week.

| you'll need |

Three nonstick mini muffin tins or a 9 by 13-inch baking dish or pan

4 cups chocolate-flavored crisp puffed rice cereal

1/2 cup packed light brown sugar

1/2 cup light corn syrup

1/2 cup creamy or crunchy peanut butter

4 ounces semi-sweet chocolate, melted

icebox **pinwheel cookies**

MAKES 7 DOZEN COOKIES

Once you make the easy chocolate and vanilla doughs, which get rolled into spiraled logs for these slice-and-bake refrigerator cookies, you can have delicious homemade treats ready at a moment's notice. To make the cookies even fancier, roll the whole log in coarse sugar before you put them in the refrigerator to chill. After baking, the outside edge of the cookies will be jewel-like with sugar crystals.

3 cups all-purpose flour

$1/2$ teaspoon baking powder

$1/2$ teaspoon salt

2 ounces unsweetened chocolate, chopped

1 cup (2 sticks) unsalted butter, softened

$1\frac{1}{3}$ cups sugar

2 large eggs

2 teaspoons pure vanilla extract

| do-aheads |

*The logs can be kept in the refrigerator for up to 2 days or in the freezer for up to 1 month.

**Store in an airtight container. They are best eaten within 2 days.

| you'll need |

Parchment paper

Ruler

Cookie sheet

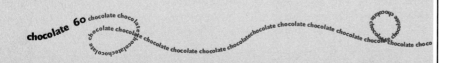

chocolate 60 chocolate chocolate chocolate chocolate chocolate chocolate chocolate chocolate chocolate chocolate chocolate chocolate chocolate choco

Sift the flour with the baking powder and salt and set aside.

Melt the chocolate in a heat-proof bowl set over a pan of simmering (but not boiling) water.

In a mixer fitted with the paddle attachment, beat the butter with the sugar on medium speed until light and fluffy, 3 to 5 minutes. With the mixer on low speed add the eggs one at a time and then add the vanilla. Add the dry ingredients and mix until just combined. Remove half of the dough and set aside. Add the melted chocolate to the remaining dough in the mixer and stir on low until combined.

Remove the dough from the mixer and shape both pieces of dough into 4 by 4-inch squares (use a ruler to measure). Wrap in plastic and refrigerate for 30 minutes.

Cut each dough square into 4 rectangular 1 by 4-inch strips. Working with one piece of dough at a time and keeping the rest refrigerated, put a piece of chocolate dough between two pieces of parchment paper and roll out into a rectangle 6 by 7 inches. Peel off the top parchment and set the dough (still on the bottom parchment) off to the side. Using 2 more pieces of parchment, roll a piece of vanilla dough out into a 6 by 6-inch square. Peel off the top parchment and flip the vanilla dough and the bottom piece of parchment onto the chocolate so that $1/2$-inch of chocolate dough is visible on both ends. Press the two doughs together lightly with a cake pan or other flat pan. Peel off the top piece of parchment and at one end fold the $1/2$ inch of overhanging chocolate dough up and over the vanilla dough. Using the bottom parchment as an aid, lift up and roll the dough into a tight pinwheel log. Remove the parchment and wrap well in plastic wrap. Put in the refrigerator for 4 to 5 hours, rotating the log a couple of times during the first hour so it doesn't develop a flat side. Repeat the procedure with the remaining dough to make 4 logs.*

Preheat the oven to 350°F.

Unwrap a log and slice it $1/4$ inch thick. Place the slices $1\frac{1}{2}$ inches apart on a lightly greased cookie sheet and bake for 9 to 11 minutes, until the vanilla part of the cookies is very light golden brown. Let cool on a rack.**

lily's **marble cake**

As a kid I used to cut through the yards to go over to my friend Lauren Shay's house. Her dad is Art Shay, the famous photographer who photographed me for *Life* magazine when I was six. When Lauren's grandma Lily stayed with them she'd always make this incredibly irresistible, just-what-it-should-be, fine-crumbed chocolate marble cake. I'll never forget how deliciously moist it was and how, remarkably, it got even better the second day. I tried to get the recipe from Lauren's mom, Florence, but she wouldn't share it. When I became a professional pastry chef I tried to re-create it, longing for that taste and texture. Frustrated that I was unable to get it just right, I contacted the family again but they still were holding on tight to it. I've been trying to get this recipe from Lauren's mother for forty years. She finally shared it with me as my wedding gift (after much badgering by her husband, her children, and her grandchildren). Now the recipe won't be lost forever. Eternal life through baking, I always say. And Lily's secret ingredient? Canned coconut. Shhh!

| do-ahead |
*The cake keeps well, covered, at room temperature for up to 4 days and is actually best after sitting overnight.

| you'll need |
10-inch tube pan

- 2½ cups all-purpose flour
- 1 tablespoon baking powder
- 1 cup whole milk
- 1 teaspoon pure vanilla extract
- 1 cup (2 sticks) unsalted butter, softened
- 2 cups sugar
- ½ teaspoon salt
- 4 large eggs
- ¼ cup cocoa powder, preferably Dutch-processed
- 1 (6-ounce) can shredded, sweetened coconut

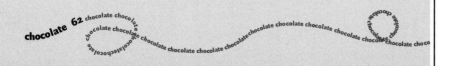

Preheat the oven to 350°F. Butter and flour a 10-inch tube pan. In a medium bowl, whisk together the flour and baking powder. In a measuring cup, combine the milk and vanilla. Set aside.

In a mixer fitted with a paddle attachment, beat the butter until light and fluffy, 3 to 5 minutes. Add the sugar and salt and continue to mix well for about 3 more minutes. Add the eggs one at a time, mixing well to combine after each addition. Alternately add the milk mixture and the flour mixture in 3 additions. Continue mixing for 5 minutes (beating a long time is important here).

Stir one third of the batter into the cocoa powder in a medium bowl. Stir the coconut into the remaining golden batter. Pour the golden batter into the prepared pan, then drop large dollops of the chocolate batter into it. Cut through the batter once or twice with a table knife to make a chocolate marble pattern. Do not stir.

Bake for 1 hour 15 minutes or until a skewer or toothpick inserted in the center comes out clean. Let cool in the pan. Invert onto a platter (for the best taste, cover with plastic wrap and let sit overnight).* Slice into wedges for serving.

individual **chocolate pavlovas**

Pavlovas are ethereal meringues, crunchy on the outside and slightly chewy on the inside. While debate rages among Australians and New Zealanders about who first invented it, both countries acknowledge that the dessert is named for the famous ballerina Anna Pavlova. Said to resemble her tutu, pavlovas are traditionally served topped with an assortment of fruit, usually berries, kiwis (to replicate the special green costume she "floated" in), and passion fruit. This is my version, made fudgy with cocoa powder, which comes out of the oven with a slightly brownie-like interior. These individual pavlovas are great for dinner parties because the bases keep well, making them perfect for an impressive, easy-to-throw-together-at-the-last-minute dessert.

| do-aheads |

*The meringues can be made up to 5 days ahead and stored in an airtight container at room temperature.

**Once assembled the pavlovas can be refrigerated for up to 2 hours before serving. (They'll lose their crispness and get chewier as they sit.)

| you'll need |

Cookie sheet

Parchment paper

Pastry bag with a large (1/2-inch) plain tip

$1/2$ cup large egg whites (from 4 to 5 eggs), at room temperature

$1/8$ teaspoon cream of tartar

$1/8$ teaspoon salt

1 cup plus 2 tablespoons sugar

$1 1/2$ teaspoons cornstarch

1 teaspoon pure vanilla extract

1 tablespoon raspberry vinegar or red wine vinegar

$1/4$ cup cocoa powder, preferably Dutch-processed, sifted

1 cup heavy cream

10 ripe strawberries, trimmed and sliced, or $1/2$ cup raspberries, blueberries, or blackberries

2 to 3 ripe kiwis, peeled and thinly sliced

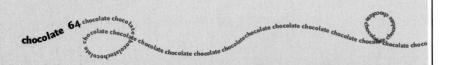

Center a rack in the oven and preheat the oven to 300°F.

In a mixer fitted with the whisk attachment, whip the egg whites, cream of tartar, and salt on medium-high speed until foamy. Add 1 cup of the sugar, the cornstarch, vanilla, and vinegar and continue whipping until the whites form stiff peaks and are smooth and shiny, about 5 minutes more. Add the cocoa powder and stir on low speed until just blended (I count to ten).

Line a cookie sheet with parchment. Fit a pastry bag with a large (½-inch) plain tip and fill the bag with the meringue. Pipe twelve 4- to 5-inch disks of meringue about 1 inch apart onto the parchment.

Bake for 40 minutes, or until the pavlovas are crisp on the outside but still moist on the inside. Remove from the oven and let them cool on the pan.*

To serve, whip the cream with the remaining 2 tablespoons sugar. Place a dollop of cream on each meringue, spreading it to the edge, and arrange the fruit on top.**

milk chocolate star anise
crème brûlée spoonfuls

MAKES 20 TO 30 SPOONFULS

I make this lovely little crème brûlée for dessert parties at the restaurant when we pass the desserts on trays like hors d'oeuvres. People are forever asking me which one of my books has this recipe and I'm always replying "the next one." So finally, here it is. Using iced tea spoons makes these look so elegant and gives the right ratio of crunchy caramelized sugar to smooth milk chocolate custard. Ceramic Asian soup spoons would work too.

Center a rack in the oven and preheat the oven to 300°F. Have ready a 9-inch baking pan set into a larger baking dish.

In a medium saucepan, heat the cream, half-and-half, vanilla bean (if using extract, you'll add it later), and star anise over medium heat and bring just to a boil. Immediately turn off the heat and add the two chocolates, whisking to melt. Set aside to infuse the flavors for 10 minutes.

Bring a tea kettle or a medium saucepan of water to a boil.

| do-aheads |

*The custard can be made up to 3 days in advance and kept in the refrigerator.

**The spoons can be prepared with the custard up to 24 hours before broiling and serving; refrigerate until needed.

| you'll need |

9-inch baking pan (preferably not aluminum) plus a larger baking dish

20 to 30 long-handled iced tea spoons or ceramic Asian soup spoons

Propane or butane kitchen torch (optional)

Cookie sheet

1 cup heavy cream

1/3 cup half-and-half

1/4 vanilla bean, halved lengthwise, or 1/8 teaspoon pure vanilla extract

1 piece star anise

1/2 ounce unsweetened chocolate, chopped

1 ounce semi-sweet chocolate, chopped

4 large egg yolks

1/4 cup granulated sugar

1/4 cup coarse sugar, raw sugar, or Demerara sugar

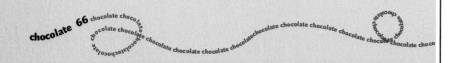

vanilla chocolate & vanilla chocolate & v
late & vanilla chocola
nilla chocolate & vanil
& vanilla chocolate & v
a chocolate & vanilla
ate & vanilla chocolat
vanilla chocolate & va
illa chocolate & vanill
colate & vanilla choco
illa chocolate & vanill
vanilla chocolate & vanill
lla chocolate & vanill

chocolate & vanilla chocolate & vanilla chocolate & vanilla chocolate & vanilla chocolate & vanilla chocolate & vanilla chocolate & vanilla chocolate & vanilla chocolate & vanilla chocolate & vanilla chocolate & vanilla chocolate & vanilla chocolate & vanilla chocolate & vanilla chocolate & vanilla chocolate & vanilla chocolate & vanilla

la chocolate & vanilla choco

Also by Gale Gand

Gale Gand's Short and Sweet (and Julia Moskin)

Gale Gand's Just a Bite (and Julia Moskin)

Butter Sugar Flour Eggs (Rick Tramonto and Julia Moskin)

American Brasserie (Rick Tramonto with Julia Moskin)

chocolate & vanilla

| gale gand with Lisa Weiss

Clarkson Potter/Publishers
New York

Published in the United States by Clarkson Potter/Publishers,
an imprint of the Crown Publishing Group,
a division of Random House, Inc., New York.
www.crownpublishing.com
www.clarksonpotter.com

Clarkson N. Potter is a trademark and Potter and colophon
are registered trademarks of Random House, Inc.

Library of Congress Cataloging-in-Publication Data
Gand, Gale.
    Chocolate and vanilla / Gale Gand with Lisa Weiss.
      p.   cm.
1. Cookery (Chocolate).   2. Cookery (Vanilla).   I. Weiss, Lisa, 1951–   II. Title.
TX767.C5G36   2006
641.6'374—dc22   2006002988

ISBN-13: 978-0-307-23852-8
ISBN-10: 0-307-23852-0

Printed in the United States of America

Design by Laura Palese

10   9   8   7   6   5   4   3   2   1

First Edition

This book is dedicated to my darling family: my sweet, loving husband, Jimmy Seidita; son, Gio Gand Tramonto; and new, twin daughters, Ella and Ruby Gand Seidita, who were kicking inside of me as I started writing this book. You all give me a reason to cook and bake and I love it. Thank you for making my life the one I dreamt of having.

vanilla

vanillavanillavanillavanillavanillavanillavanillavanillavanil
llavanillavanillavanillavanillavanillavanillavanillavanillava
vanillavanillavanillavanillavanillavanillavanillavanillavanil

VANILLA EXTRACT

Introduction to Vanilla

I like to think of vanilla as the "underwear of baking." What I *really* mean is that I see vanilla like an invisible essential, something that's always in the background, the thing you put on before anything else. Maybe I should start referring to it as "lingerie," since vanilla can also be quite seductive. As a supporting player, vanilla balances, mellows, and gives depth to everything from chocolate chip cookies to apple pie and brownies, without announcing its presence. But when it's a star, say in ice cream or vanilla custard, it becomes sexy and alluring, and even shyly assertive.

I often wonder how such an incredibly exotic and sought-after ingredient became just another word for bland. I think it might have something to do with the fact that it has suffered from comparison to its natural—and often dominating—partner, chocolate. What I know for certain is that I've been under vanilla's intoxicating spell my whole life.

During my childhood in the late 1950s and early 1960s, Deerfield Bakery in Deerfield, Illinois, was *the* bakery for every important occasion in town—birthdays, weddings, bar mitzvahs, christenings, and anniversaries. Every Saturday morning I looked forward to a trip there with my mom to buy butter-crust bread for the week and cookies by the pound, though all I could think about were vanilla cupcakes: rows and rows of golden cupcakes topped with swirls of white frosting and sprinkles. And I got to pick one and have it all to myself! The idea of miniature cakes always delighted me because they were individual and I didn't have to share with my older brother—and I could lick all the icing off first if I wanted to. There were chocolate cupcakes too, but it was really the vanilla ones I went for, the aroma of vanilla beckoning to me from the moment I stepped through the bakery door; actually vanilla wafted throughout my entire hometown of Deerfield, because Sara Lee Bakery's main plant and headquarters were there.

As a professional pastry chef for over twenty years, I like to think of vanilla as an old friend. But when I went to work on this book, I thought maybe I had begun to take my old friend for granted. At Tru, the fine-dining restaurant I co-own in Chicago, we go through gallons of vanilla extract and tens of pounds of vanilla beans yearly. I conduct tastings of various vanilla beans for my staff, but I had to ask myself what I really knew about this ingredient that plays such an indispensable role in the sweet

kitchen. I decided to learn a bit more—not just about the extract sitting in that little brown bottle on nearly every American pantry shelf, but about the history and manufacture of those tropical vanilla beans themselves.

What's intrigued me the most was finding out that the "manufacture" of vanilla is actually completed long before the beans leave the rain forest where they're grown and is accomplished by the same methods the ancient indigenous people of the Americas used at least 2,000 years ago. Even turning beans into aromatic extract (as I found out when touring the largest sole manufacturing plant of pure vanilla extract in the country, the Nielsen-Massey plant in Waukegan, Illinois, not far from my home-town of Deerfield) is an amazingly quiet, simple, low-tech procedure. The ultimate quality of the fin-ished extract depends as much on the care taken during the long curing process at the beans' point of origin, as it does on the extraction process. Now, whether I'm in the restaurant pastry kitchen or my kitchen at home, every time I pick up a vanilla bean, or reach for that bottle of extract, I think about the millennia-long journey the only edible fruit of the orchid plant has taken to become one of the most sought-after—and expensive—flavors in the world.

When I'm looking for a dessert to make, I like to think first in terms of flavor—"Do I have a taste for chocolate or vanilla?"—not whether I want a cake or ice cream. So if you have a yen for vanilla, I've divided the recipes into two flavor categories: those that use vanilla beans, and those that use pure vanilla extract. When you use whole beans in your dessert, you'll end up with a more intense vanilla fla-vor, like in the Crème Anglaise with Peaches and Berries, or the Buttermilk Panna Cotta with Strawberry Mash. (You can even narrow it down to Tahitian, Bourbon, Mexican, or Indonesian vanilla beans, which all have distinct flavor profiles.) These are the slightly more refined recipes of the bunch. Recipes that call for vanilla extract are a little more subtle in their vanilla flavor, since extract is usually added in small amounts before a dessert is baked, or it's used to enhance other flavors like fruit or chocolate.

None of the recipes included in this book are complicated or require any fancy pastry-chef techniques. In fact, many are downright easy—even for beginners—for instance the Cherries in Port over Vanilla Ice Cream, or the Vanilla Butter Caramels. But if you're looking for an afternoon project, go to the Éclairs with Coffee Glaze or the Vanilla Charlotte: They might require more time in the kitchen, but neither recipe is difficult. Really none of them are. They're all recipes I use at home.

Almost all of the recipes I've chosen to feature hold special memories for me—like my mom's Vanilla Malteds, my mother-in-law Vita's Ricotta Doughnuts, and the Late-Night Vanilla Flan I made with my son, Gio. Some are classics I couldn't resist tweaking a little bit, like the Vanilla-Scented Peach Tarte Tatin, Vanilla Raspberry Rice Pudding, or the Boston Cream Cupcakes I made for my restaurant partner Rich Melman. But others, like the Crème Légère with Macerated Peaches or the Limoncello Strawberries with Sour Cream and Vanilla Sugar, are incredibly simple and could end up being your family's new favorite.

Whether you want to quickly indulge your last-minute craving, or are looking for a pull-out-all-the-stops vanilla dessert for a celebration meal, dust off that bottle of vanilla extract, or grab that vanilla bean you've been keeping in the pantry. I know you'll find a recipe in these pages to inspire you. So call vanilla soothing, or comforting maybe, but please, just don't call it plain.

A Brief History of the Vanilla Bean

As a child, whenever I would dab vanilla extract behind my ears and on my wrist, just like my mom did with her fancy passion-flower perfume, I was convinced that I was the first person in the world to have discovered vanilla's irresistible scent. Even now I admit to having been just a tad surprised when I learned that vanilla's intoxicating aroma was discovered *at least 2,000 years ago* by the Totonacs, an ancient people living in southeastern Mexico.

It makes me wonder, though, just how they figured out that an *odorless* plump green pod from an orchid could be turned into a svelte, dark, and exquisitely *fragrant* vanilla bean. It's a culinary mystery, I guess, sort of like which brave person first ate a raw oyster, or who discovered that a thorny thistle contained the exquisite meat of an artichoke heart.

At any rate, the Aztecs, who conquered the Totonacs and learned from them how to cultivate and cure the orchid, are usually given credit for discovering vanilla, when what they really did was popularize its use throughout most of Mexico and Central America by using it to enhance their favorite, very bitter, hot drink: *chocolatl*.

When Spanish conquistador Hernando Cortés arrived in Mexico in 1519, he was wined and dined by the emperor Montezuma II, then was served a warm chocolate after-dinner drink that was laced with honey

and spices and aromatic with the scent of vanilla. Cortés must have been pretty surprised when he caught a whiff of vanilla in his drink, because although the beans had been taken back to Spain some fifteen years earlier from the New World, Europeans at the time thought that vanilla was strictly a perfume.

Cortés acquired quite a taste for the Aztecs' chocolate drink, and when he returned to Spain, cacao (*ka-kow*) and vanilla beans were included in his cache of plundered gold, silver, and gems. At first his fellow Spaniards must have thought Cortés had gone a little *loco* because they didn't think a drink of bitter chocolate paste mixed with spicy chilies was particularly tasty; but they *were* seduced by the gentle alluring flavor of the vanilla that was also added to the drink.

By the early 1600s the exotic new chocolate drink flavored with vanilla (and eventually with sugar) was the rage among the upper class of Europe. Queen Elizabeth I adored vanilla, though we don't know whether she was simply indulging her reputedly voracious sweet tooth, or believed the advice of her apothecary, Hugh Morgan, who extolled vanilla's health benefits. No matter, Mr. Morgan made the absolutely brilliant suggestion—he also just happened to be her pastry chef (everyone should have one, don't you think?)—that vanilla could be used as a flavor on its own, in pastries and custards and not just as a partner to chocolate. It was a defining moment in the history of desserts.

However, by the late 1600s vanilla began to fall out of vogue with the Spanish, who preferred flavoring their chocolate with cinnamon because it was cheaper and more available. Meanwhile, the use of vanilla increased in Italy and France. The French loved vanilla so much, in fact, that they began looking for ways to increase their vanilla supplies and in the early part of the 1800s transported cuttings of the vine to their colonies on the Bourbon (*Boor*-bon) Islands in the Indian Ocean. (The name Bourbon comes from a French royal family and has nothing to do with whiskey.) Disappointingly the blossoms failed to produce fruit. It wasn't until 1836 that a botanist from Belgium, Charles Morren, realized that the cultivated orchids were not self-pollinating and needed a little "fertility assistance," which in Mexico was accomplished by indigenous Melipone bees and hummingbirds, species that were physically (and uniquely) equipped for the task. With no access to these reliable little helpers, Morren devised a brilliant but tedious method of hand-pollination. Finally, in 1841, Edmond Albius, a former slave on the Bourbon Island of Réunion, came to the rescue of all future vanilla lovers when

he perfected a quick and efficient way to hand-pollinate the orchid using a short, thin bamboo skewer, a method still used today.

Vanilla made its debut in the United States in 1789 when our ambassador to France, Thomas Jefferson, had his secretary in Paris ship him a bundle of fifty cured beans wrapped in newspaper. It's not hard to guess how he used them; Thomas Jefferson's recipe for vanilla ice cream can be found in his papers at the Library of Congress.

In the beginning of the 1800s everyone started screaming for ice cream, and in 1837 Joseph Burnett, a pharmacist in Boston, invented a method for extracting the flavor from whole vanilla beans, making vanilla much easier to use. Today, Americans annually consume an amazing 2,000 tons of vanilla, more than half of the world's supply, with most of it going to the soft-drink (think Coke and Pepsi), ice cream (of course), and—I like to think thanks to me—perfume industries.

From Pod to Bean How Vanilla Is Made

So just how *does* that odorless plump green pod turn svelte, dark, chewy, and exquisitely fragrant? The simple answer is with a great deal of patience and a lot of work—a lot of hard work.

Vanilla is the most labor-intensive agricultural product in the world and second only to saffron in expense. To give you an example, in 2003 when vanilla prices were at an all-time high because tropical storms had wiped out entire plantations, the retail cost of a pound of saffron was around $1,000 and a pound of Madagascar vanilla beans was going for about $750 retail. In 2005 the cost of Madagascar vanilla beans was closer to "normal" at $150 a pound retail.

Vanilla beans are the cured seedpods of large orchid vines, which, like cacao trees, grow in a tropical belt that extends roughly 20 to 25 degrees north and south of the equator. Of the 25,000 or so varieties of orchids in the world, only three species (*Vanilla planifolia* or *fragrans, Vanilla pompona,* and *Vanilla tahitiensis*) produce edible fruit. Left untended in the wild, vanilla vines can grow to fifty feet tall, but on plantations they are kept within reach of human hands for harvesting by looping the vines over stakes or specially planted trees.

From the time a cutting is planted under a canopy of rain-forest trees, it must receive just the right amount of sunlight and shade, heat and humidity to produce blossoms, a process that can take up to three years. Then once the pretty pale yellow-green flowers make their early-morning appearance, if they're not pollinated by midafternoon, they wither and fall from the vine like dejected spinsters. Luckily for the workers who have to pollinate the blossoms by hand—up to a thousand on one vine —the flowers don't appear all at the same time, but that also means the vines need to be inspected daily. Each fertilized flower produces just one large (six- to ten-inch) green-bean-like seed pod that takes seven to nine months to ripen to a stage where it can be harvested.

After the mature pods are harvested (again by hand) they begin a four- to six-month curing process. It varies a little depending on where they're grown, but there are basically four steps to the method. First the pods are given a brief dip in boiling water to halt the ripening process. Then they're laid out to dry in the sun by day and swaddled in blankets or straw mats at night. Day after day the drying and sweating process is repeated until the fermented beans are ready for "conditioning," where they're placed on racks or grass mats for a couple of months to develop their fragrance and flavor. From there the wrinkled, dark brown vanilla beans are sorted, graded, and shipped to markets around the world. It takes five pounds of pods to make about one pound of cured beans.

The majority of vanilla beans end up as extract. Pure vanilla extract is made in a way that is similar to percolating coffee, where all the flavor is coaxed out of chopped vanilla beans as a mixture of ethyl alcohol and water is pumped through them. Most extract is made with heated liquid (about 130°F) to quicken the process, but better manufacturers use cold-water extraction (75°F or below), which retains more of the beans' flavor and fragrance. The cold-water process takes about forty-eight hours; then the mixture is placed in holding tanks for anywhere from a few days to several weeks to age before finally being filtered and bottled.

Buying Vanilla

Like that of its tropical cousins, coffee and chocolate, the flavor and fragrance of vanilla varies according to where it's grown. Differences in soil, climate, and curing processes result in beans that have distinct flavor profiles and again, as with coffee and chocolate, preference all comes down to a matter

As with any valuable commodity, vanilla has often been the target of thieves. For years many growers have used needles to "tattoo" special markings on the green pods which remain after the beans had been cured, which allows them to be identified if they're stolen and then recovered. In the last few years, as vanilla prices soared, plantation owners, buyers, and dealers have taken protective measures against theft, with armed guards and elaborate ruses and disguises for buying and then transporting vanilla beans.

of personal taste. Although vanilla is produced in eight tropical regions of the world, these are the four most important ones:

- **Madagascar Bourbon Vanilla** Madagascar is one of the Bourbon Islands along with the Comoro Islands, Réunion Island (formerly called the Île de Bourbon), and the Seychelles Islands in the Indian Ocean off the east coast of Africa. The French planted cuttings there from the Mexican vanilla orchid, and now nearly eighty percent of the world's vanilla comes from this region. Madagascar beans are considered to be the best quality of all the varieties. They are creamy, sweet, and rich, while beans from the other Bourbon islands can have spicy notes.

- **Indonesian Vanilla** After Madagascar, Indonesia has become the world's second largest producer of vanilla. In the past, because they were picked early and then quickly cured over open fire, the beans had a smoky, harsh quality. Now, growers are curing the beans slowly and the quality has improved immensely. It's rare, though not impossible (see Sources, Chocolate page 79) to find whole Indonesian beans because most are blended with Bourbon beans for extract.

- **Mexican Vanilla** Although Mexico once had a three-hundred-year monopoly on vanilla production, up until recently Mexican vanilla beans grew scarce because many vanilla plantations had been replaced by more lucrative crops and oil fields, and the beans that were produced were of inconsistent quality. The good news is that in the past few years growers have worked to revive the industry. Mexican vanilla beans are wonderfully creamy, sweet, and spicy, with hints of clove and nutmeg, and many connoisseurs consider Mexican vanilla to be the finest vanilla of all.

- **Tahitian Vanilla** Tahitian vanilla orchids originally came from the same stock as the indigenous Mexican orchid but mutated in the wild to form an entirely new species. While the beans are shorter and plumper than Madagascar or Mexican, their thicker pod walls mean they have fewer

seeds. Tahitian vanilla tastes sweet and fruity like cherries and has a pronounced floral fragrance that many vanilla lovers prize.

WHOLE VANILLA BEANS

I like to buy whole vanilla beans that I can see and feel, so I usually look for them loose rather than in individual glass jars (see Sources, Chocolate page 79). If that's all you can find, make sure your purveyor is reliable and has a good turnover. Good vanilla beans are glossy, dark, and, most importantly, supple. You should almost be able to wind a bean around your finger. Pass on any that are stiff or brittle. If you happen to find beans that appear to be dusted with sugar crystals, scoop them up— they're prizewinners. That white stuff is vanillin, the natural substance that gives the bean its flavor.

PURE VANILLA EXTRACT

Pure vanilla extract captures the essence of the bean in a bottle and I use only pure vanilla extract in my recipes. Although fragrance and flavor can vary according to the manufacturer, by law, any vanilla extract labeled "pure" can contain sugar, corn syrup, caramel, or color but must contain at least thirty-five percent alcohol. Manufacturers are not required to state percentages of sugar added, but labels must list all the ingredients. Sugar is added as a stabilizer and better grades have less sugar while some extracts need more to mask inferior flavor. A good rule of thumb is that the better the brand, the fewer ingredients added, and frankly, you get what you pay for. Pure vanilla made from premium beans is expensive but worth it in the long run; a little goes a long way in flavor dividends. While supermarket vanillas are usually blends of different beans and can be quite good, the best brands are single-origin beans and specify the country on their labels (see Sources, Chocolate page 79).

Natural vanilla flavoring (sometimes called pure vanilla flavoring) is made from vanilla beans without or with very little alcohol. It's an acceptable substitute for those who avoid alcoholic products but is less flavorful than vanilla extract.

Imitation vanilla is just that: a man-made chemical compound that poorly mimics the flavor and aroma of real vanilla. It's manufactured from paper industry by-products or coal tar and has a harsh, bitter aftertaste. You can probably guess that I don't recommend it. To make it a little more

confusing, there's also **vanillin flavoring,** which is a blend of natural and imitation vanilla, but why bother when the real stuff is so much better?

VANILLA PASTE

Recipes often call for whole vanilla beans and then instruct you to cut the bean in half lengthwise and scrape out the gooey vanilla seeds, or "vanilla caviar," as I like to call it. (Most of my recipes are the exception; see Working with Vanilla, Whole Beans, below.) With paste, the vanilla seeds are suspended in a viscous liquid to be spooned out as needed; the scraping is done for you and will save you a step in the kitchen. Vanilla paste usually comes in a dark brown jar to protect it from its natural enemy, light. One tablespoon of paste equals about 1 scraped bean or 1 tablespoon extract.

VANILLA POWDER

I first learned about vanilla powder when I went to pastry school in Paris. Recently it has become available in the United States in some upscale markets or by mail order (see Sources, Chocolate page 79). Made from dried and powdered pure Madagascar beans and combined with a base of malto-dextrin, it has no sugar or alcohol and can be used in any recipe calling for vanilla, substituted in equal proportions (1 tablespoon powder equals 1 bean or 1 tablespoon extract). I like to add it to baked goods along with the other dry ingredients.

Working with Vanilla

Vanilla can be purchased in several forms, all of which are pretty much interchangeable. Generally— and since they're so expensive—I like to use whole beans to infuse into liquids and when I want to "show off" the vanilla beans' particular flavor, or want to see the specks of vanilla caviar in custards or mousses. Vanilla extract is perfect for baked goods, say cakes and cookies, when the flavor of vanilla is more subtle and it's not important to see those distinctive black specks of the seeds. Extract is much more convenient to use than whole beans because it mixes more easily, and if you're concerned, the alcohol evaporates during cooking.

WHOLE BEANS

- Many cookbook authors direct you to split your vanilla bean lengthwise and then scrape the beans from the halves before adding them to a mixture. I'm different. I almost never *scrape* the seeds from

the bean, mainly because I dislike the little "threads" that come off the pod when you scrape the seeds. I just add the split vanilla bean to the liquid and the seeds release on their own just fine. As an added bonus, once you've infused a vanilla bean into liquid, the bean can be removed, rinsed, and stored in the refrigerator to be used a few more times. It's not a one-shot deal, but continues to give off flavor three to four more times. Even when it seems to have finally been exhausted, it can still be plunged into sugar to make vanilla sugar (below) or vanilla brandy (page 20).

- To store whole vanilla beans, wrap them tightly in plastic or aluminum foil and then place in a resealable plastic bag. They will keep in a cool, dark cupboard for at least six months. (Not the refrigerator, though, please. It causes condensation that in turn encourages the growth of mold.) I've heard that well-stored beans can last for three or four years, but how could a baker go so long without using them?

- If the beans become dry, all is not lost. If you're using them in custard, once you steep them in the hot liquid they'll soften again. If not, put the dry beans in an airtight container with some sugar and, ta-da, in a few days the aroma and flavor of vanilla will have permeated the sugar. Vanilla sugar can be used for sprinkling on finished baked goods or used to flavor whipped cream.

VANILLA EXTRACT

- Both direct and indirect light cause the fragrance and flavor from vanilla extract to dissipate and that's why it comes in dark brown bottles. Keep it tightly capped in a cool, dark cupboard and it will last indefinitely.

MAKING SUBSTITUTIONS

Seeds from 1 whole bean equal about 1 tablespoon vanilla extract

Seeds from 1 (2-inch) piece of a vanilla bean equal about 1 teaspoon vanilla extract

1 tablespoon pure vanilla paste equals about 1 vanilla bean or 1 tablespoon vanilla extract

1 tablespoon pure vanilla powder equals about 1 tablespoon vanilla extract

sour cream ice cream

MAKES ABOUT 1 QUART, OR 8 SERVINGS

The sour cream in this oh-so-easy recipe lends a subtle tanginess to what would otherwise be just "plain old" vanilla ice cream. It makes a natural partner for berries in the spring and stone fruits in the summer, as well as apple and caramel desserts in the fall and winter.

In a bowl, whisk together the sour cream, half-and-half, lemon juice, sugar, and vanilla bean or extract and let the mixture get cold in the refrigerator for at least 1 hour.*

Whisk the mixture one more time and then remove the vanilla bean. Transfer to the bowl of an ice cream maker and freeze according to the manufacturer's instructions. Transfer to a container with a lid and freeze for at least 2 more hours.**

| do-aheads |

*You can make the ice cream base as much as 3 days in advance, cover it, and keep it refrigerated. Just give it a good stir one last time before freezing it.

**The ice cream is best eaten the same day, but it can be kept frozen for about 3 days. Let the ice cream soften slightly at room temperature for 10 minutes before serving if it seems too hard to scoop.

| you'll need |

Ice cream maker

2 cups sour cream

1 cup half-and-half

2 tablespoons freshly squeezed lemon juice

1 cup plus 2 tablespoons sugar

1/2 vanilla bean, halved lengthwise, or 1/2 tablespoon vanilla paste, or 1 1/2 teaspoons pure vanilla extract

cherries in port over vanilla ice cream

MAKES 4 TO 6 SERVINGS

I love making this recipe because it is really easy and it contains no added sugar; its sweetness comes from reduced and intensified port flavored with vanilla bean. (Try a Tahitian vanilla bean if you can; its floral aroma marries really well with cherries.) The sauce is wonderful served simply over good vanilla ice cream or Sour Cream Ice Cream (opposite), but try it over fresh whole-milk ricotta or frozen yogurt for a lighter choice. Door County in Wisconsin is my local source for fresh sour cherries, but frozen sour cherries are just fine. I try to go up there each summer with my dad to go to a fish boil (with fresh perch), eat Swedish pancakes with lingonberries, play folk music, and pick up some pies, in the village of Fish Creek, from my favorite pie shop, Sweetie Pies.

Put the port, cinnamon stick, and vanilla bean in a heavy medium saucepan; bring to a simmer over medium heat; and let cook until the liquid is reduced to 1 cup, 20 to 30 minutes.

Add the cherries and cook until they're just heated through, about 1 minute.

Blend the cornstarch with the reserved cherry juice and then stir it into the port and cherries. (If you used fresh cherries, remove some of the reduction, let it cool, and then mix it with the cornstarch.) Reduce the heat to low and cook just until the mixture has thickened, about 2 minutes.

Remove from the heat and let cool a little.* Serve warm over scoops of vanilla ice cream.

| do-ahead |

*The cherries can be served at room temperature or refrigerated for up to 3 days and reheated before serving.

3 cups ruby port

1 cinnamon stick

½ vanilla bean, halved lengthwise

2 cups frozen sour cherries, thawed and drained (juice reserved), or fresh pitted sour cherries

1 tablespoon cornstarch

1 pint vanilla ice cream

frozen poppy-seed mousse
with **vanilla-poached stone fruit**

MAKES 8 SERVINGS

I think I have a genetic predisposition (from my Hungarian grandparents) that attracts me to anything with poppy seeds. This sliceable loaf of frozen vanilla mousse, kind of like airy vanilla-brandy ice cream, is a great do-ahead dessert. The vanilla's flavor is subtle enough not to fight with the hard-to-put-your-finger-on flavor of the poppy seeds. I also love the contrast of the cold mousse against warm poached stone fruit.

Although vanilla brandy can be purchased, I've found that making my own is a great way to recycle used vanilla beans and I'm continually adding them to a big Mason jar at the restaurant. To make your own vanilla brandy, put several rinsed and dried vanilla beans together with a 750-milliliter bottle of brandy in a Mason jar. You can add more vanilla beans as they're used and more brandy to keep them covered.

A narrow ceramic terrine mold (mine is Le Creuset and 11½ by 3½ by 2½ inches deep) works well for the frozen mousse, but a five-cup nonaluminum loaf pan will work, too.

for the mousse
4 large egg yolks
½ cup sugar
2 tablespoons honey
6 tablespoons milk
6 tablespoons vanilla brandy or cognac
2 heaping tablespoons poppy seeds
½ vanilla bean, halved lengthwise
1¾ cups heavy cream

for the poached stone fruit
4 cups water
1 cup sugar
½ vanilla bean, halved lengthwise
1 (3-inch) strip lemon zest
2 ripe apricots, quartered and pitted
2 ripe peaches, halved, pitted, and cut into eighths, or pitted and cut into 8 wedges
2 ripe plums, quartered and pitted

| do-aheads |
*The terrine can be kept frozen for up to 2 weeks.

**The poached fruit can be made 4 days ahead and kept refrigerated.

| you'll need |
Terrine mold or nonaluminum loaf pan
Parchment paper

Line the bottom and sides of a 5-cup terrine mold or loaf pan with parchment paper (it helps to put a few dabs of butter in the pan first so the paper will stick). Bring a few inches of water to a simmer in a medium saucepan; lower the heat so the water barely simmers.

To make the mousse, in a medium stainless-steel bowl that fits on top of the saucepan without touching the water, whisk the egg yolks with the sugar, honey, milk, brandy, poppy seeds, and vanilla bean until combined. Set the bowl over the simmering water and whisk the mixture continuously until it's thickened and hot to the touch, 10 to 15 minutes. Remove this custard base from the heat and set aside to cool, stirring occasionally. Remove the vanilla bean.

Whip the cream until it holds stiff peaks. Fold the whipped cream into the custard, then pour the mousse into the prepared mold and smooth out the surface with a spatula. Cover with plastic wrap and freeze for at least 6 hours or better yet, overnight.

Remove the mold from the freezer, turn the mousse out onto a work surface, and remove the parchment paper. (Let the mold sit at room temperature for a few minutes or dip in warm water briefly if needed to get it to release from the mold.) Wrap the mousse with plastic wrap, place it back in the mold, and return the mold to the freezer until serving.*

For the poached stone fruit, put the water, the sugar, vanilla bean, and lemon zest in a large saucepan and bring to a boil. Add the apricots, peaches, and plums; bring the liquid back to a gentle simmer; and cook for 1 minute, stirring once or twice. Turn off the heat, and then let the fruit cool in the poaching liquid. When completely cool, transfer to a covered container and refrigerate until serving.**

To serve, remove the mousse from the freezer, unwrap it, and cut it into 1-inch-thick slices (the two ends are for the chef). Rewarm the poached fruit. Cut the slices in half diagonally and place 2 triangles on each dessert plate along with a spoonful of poached fruit and some of the poaching liquid.

crème anglaise with peaches and berries

MAKES ABOUT 4 SERVINGS

If you want to have one good dessert sauce in your repertoire, make it this one: Crème anglaise is considered THE mother sauce in pastry. From this simple vanilla-infused egg-thickened elixir stems everything: Thicken it with starch to make pastry cream, freeze it to make ice cream, or use cream instead of milk to turn it into crème brûlée. I could go on and on. Premium Madagascar Bourbon beans, with their strong aroma and creamy flavor, show off best in this luscious, creamy sauce, paired here with ripe summer fruits.

| do-ahead |

*The sauce will keep for up to 3 days in the refrigerator.

| you'll need |

Instant-read thermometer, optional

2 cups whole milk

1/2 vanilla bean, halved lengthwise

6 large egg yolks

2/3 cup sugar

3 ripe peaches, pitted and cut into wedges

1/2 pint raspberries or blueberries

Have ready near your cooktop a large bowl filled three-quarters full with ice and cover the ice with water.

Bring the milk and vanilla bean almost to a boil in a large saucepan over medium-high heat. Turn off the heat and let the vanilla steep in the milk for 10 minutes.

In a medium bowl, whisk the egg yolks with the sugar for 1 minute and then gradually drizzle in the hot milk, whisking continuously.

Return the mixture to the saucepan and, stirring constantly with a wooden spoon, cook over medium heat until the sauce has thickened and registers 180°F on an instant-read thermometer, being careful not to overcook it or it will break. (If you don't have a thermometer, test it by dipping a wooden spoon into the mixture and then running your finger down the back of the spoon. If the stripe remains intact, the mixture is ready; if the edges blur, the mixture is not cooked or thick enough yet.) Immediately strain the mixture through a fine-mesh sieve into a bowl and then place that in the larger bowl of ice water. Stir occasionally until the sauce is cool and then refrigerate it in a covered container.*

To serve, place the peaches and berries in dessert bowls and pour the crème anglaise over the fruit.

buttermilk panna cotta with
strawberry mash

MAKES 8 SERVINGS

My husband, Jimmy, stops reading the dessert menu in a restaurant when he reaches the panna cotta, a creamy, easily made custard. Here's one of Jimmy's favorite versions that has the warm flavor of vanilla along with the tangy kick of buttermilk. Make sure you leave enough time to let the panna cottas chill in the fridge before you serve them.

Have ready eight 4-ounce ramekins or dessert cups.

Put the buttermilk, cream, sugar, and vanilla bean in a medium saucepan and bring the liquid to a boil.

Meanwhile, gradually sprinkle the gelatin over the cold water in a small bowl and let it sit until it's softened.

As soon as the buttermilk mixture comes to a boil, remove the saucepan from the heat and stir in the softened gelatin. Strain the mixture through a fine-mesh strainer into a large pitcher or measuring cup with a spout. Pour into the ramekins and chill in the refrigerator for at least 2 hours before serving.*

To make the strawberry mash, using a potato masher or fork, crush the strawberries with the sugar.**

Spread the strawberry mash over the surface of the chilled panna cottas just before serving.

| do-aheads |
*The panna cottas will keep, covered with plastic wrap, in the fridge for up to 3 days.
**You can mash the strawberries up to 2 hours ahead and let them sit at room temperature.

| you'll need |
Eight 4-ounce ramekins or shallow baking dishes

for the panna cotta
2 cups buttermilk
1½ cups heavy cream
½ cup plus 2 tablespoons sugar
½ vanilla bean, halved lengthwise
2 teaspoons powdered gelatin
4 teaspoons cold water

for the strawberry mash
1 pint strawberries
2 tablespoons sugar

limoncello strawberries with
sour cream and vanilla sugar

MAKES 4 SERVINGS

During about three weeks every June in the Midwest, strawberries — the kind that are red to the core and sweet, sweet, sweet — are begging to be picked and eaten or put up. My son, Gio, and I like to go in the morning with my friend Judy to Thompson's Strawberry Farm near Kenosha, Wisconsin, to pick baskets full. I love looking down the aisle of bushy berry plants and seeing Gio picking berries, repeating "one for me, one for the basket." After a lunch of bratwurst at the Brat Stop, we drive our treasure home and the house always smells like a field of strawberries (and so does the trunk of the car, for that matter).

Limoncello is a refreshing Italian digestif that's an infusion of lemon rinds into a neutral spirit like vodka. You can often find it at stores that carry imported liquor and wine, but Cointreau or another liqueur with an intense citrusy flavor can be substituted.

To make the vanilla sugar, in an airtight container, bury the vanilla bean in the sugar and let it sit overnight, the longer the better to infuse the sugar with the vanilla flavor.*

Toss the berries with the limoncello and divide among 4 small dessert bowls. Top each bowl with a spoonful of sour cream and a teaspoon or so of vanilla sugar.

| do-ahead |
*The vanilla sugar needs at least 12 hours to infuse but can be kept indefinitely. In fact, the longer the better as the vanilla bean will impart more of its flavor to the sugar as it sits.

for the vanilla sugar
- ½ vanilla bean (can be one that was previously used)
- 1 cup sugar

for the strawberries
- 1 pint strawberries, green tops trimmed off
- 1 tablespoon limoncello, Cointreau, or liqueur of your choice
- 1 cup sour cream

vanilla raspberry rice pudding
with lemon-vanilla caramel

MAKES 4 TO 6 SERVINGS

Being the custard lover that I am, I've always been fond of rice pudding, but during the time I lived in England—home of soothing nursery desserts spiked with vanilla by order of the queen—I fell in love all over again with one of my childhood favorites. Prepared stovetop with Arborio rice, the rice used in risotto, this pudding becomes extra creamy, without the use of cream. It's made more grown-up with accents of tart raspberries and a citrusy caramel syrup.

| do-aheads |

*The rice pudding can be made up to 3 days ahead and kept covered in the refrigerator.

**The caramel can be stored in the refrigerator for up to 1 week.

***The puddings can be assembled and kept refrigerated for up to 8 hours before serving.

for the rice pudding

½ cup Arborio rice

2 cups milk

¼ vanilla bean, halved lengthwise

6 tablespoons sugar

½ pint raspberries

for the lemon-vanilla caramel

¾ cup sugar

½ cup corn syrup

¾ vanilla bean, halved lengthwise

¾ cup freshly squeezed lemon juice

In a strainer, rinse the rice under cold water for 1 minute, moving it around with your hands to remove some of the starch.

To make the rice pudding, in a medium saucepan combine the rice with the milk and vanilla bean and bring to a simmer. Cook until very tender, 20 to 25 minutes. Turn off the heat and stir in the sugar.*

For the lemon-vanilla caramel, put the sugar, corn syrup, and vanilla bean in a medium high-walled saucepan (this will help protect you from the bubbling hot caramel) and bring to a boil. Cook until it turns golden amber. Using a wooden spoon, *carefully* stir in the lemon juice; the hot caramel will spatter a little at first. Once the caramel is smooth, remove it from the heat and set aside to cool. Transfer to a container and chill in the refrigerator until ready to serve.**

To serve the pudding, divide about half of the lemon-vanilla caramel among 4 to 6 stemmed glasses, and then portion half of the chilled rice pudding on top. Add the raspberries and cover them with the remaining rice pudding. Finish by covering the surface of the puddings with another layer of caramel, which will ooze down to the bottom.***

late-night **vanilla flan**

MAKES ONE 9-INCH FLAN, OR 8 TO 10 SERVINGS

I was originally going to call this "Easy Vanilla Flan" but after writing the recipe I realized it only seemed easy to me because I made thirty servings late one night with my son, Gio, for a Cinco de Mayo celebration in Mr. Jackson's third-grade class. We made it again for Rosh Hashanah with its sweet caramel syrup, instead of the traditional apples and honey, to wish all a sweet (Jewish) New Year. Though not difficult, it does have a few steps. I think it's a great do-ahead dessert because one of the steps is overnight refrigeration, plus I always have these ingredients on hand. When we make it, Gio does all the work; I'm just the conductor.

Have ready near your cooktop a 9-inch round cake pan, a baking dish large enough to fit the cake pan, and a bowl large enough to fit a deep medium saucepan. Fill the bowl halfway with ice and add enough water to cover the ice.

To make the caramel, put 2 cups of the sugar into the center of the saucepan and then slowly pour ½ cup water down and around the pan's interior walls, trying not to splash any sugar onto the sides of the pan. Do not stir the water and sugar together; instead, gently draw your finger through the center of the sugar twice, making an "X," just to moisten it, which helps keep the caramel from crystallizing.

| do-aheads |
*The caramel-coated pan can be prepared up to 3 days in advance and kept wrapped with plastic wrap at room temperature.

**The custard mixture can be refrigerated for up to 3 days before it's poured into the pan and baked. Add 15 minutes to the cooking time if the custard is cold when it goes into the oven.

***The cooked flan can be kept refrigerated for up to 48 hours before serving.

| you'll need |
9-inch round cake pan plus baking dish that holds it comfortably

3 cups sugar
½ cup water
4 cups whole milk
½ vanilla bean, halved lengthwise
7 large eggs
2 large egg yolks

Bring the water and sugar to a boil over high heat without stirring, and cook until the mixture turns an amber color, about 15 minutes. Immediately remove the saucepan from the heat and place in the bowl of ice water to stop the cooking. The caramel will sizzle a little so don't be alarmed.

Leave the pan in the ice water for 1 minute to stop the caramel cooking, then lift it out, dry the bottom of the saucepan, and quickly pour the caramel into the cake pan. Tilt the cake pan in all directions so the caramel coats the bottom and sides of the pan to the rim. Be careful as the caramel is still hot. Set the cake pan aside to cool.*

Center a rack in the oven and preheat the oven to 300°F. Bring a tea kettle or a medium saucepan of water to a boil.

Bring the milk and vanilla bean to a boil in a large saucepan over medium-high heat. As soon as it comes to a boil, turn off the heat and let the vanilla steep in the milk for 10 minutes.

In a large bowl, whisk the eggs and egg yolks with the remaining 1 cup sugar until well blended. Whisk in about ½ cup of the hot milk until well combined, then whisk in the remaining milk. Strain through a fine-mesh sieve into a pitcher or large glass measuring cup with a spout.**

Pour the custard mixture into the caramel-lined cake pan and place the pan in the baking dish. Pour boiling water into the baking dish to come halfway up the sides of the cake pan. Place the baking dish in the oven. Bake until the custard is light blond, dry on top, and set in the center, 60 to 75 minutes. It should not "shimmy" if jiggled slightly.

Turn off the oven and open the door completely to let it cool, about 1 hour. Remove the pan from the baking dish and let cool completely. Cover tightly with plastic wrap and refrigerate for at least 12 hours.***

To serve, run a table knife around the flan and place a serving platter upside down over the pan. Quickly invert the platter and pan, to turn out the flan and catch the liquid caramel. Cut the flan into wedges and serve with a spoonful of the caramel sauce that runs down the sides.

crème légère with macerated peaches

MAKES 6 TO 8 SERVINGS

This is a simple embellishment on peaches and cream—one of my favorite rewards for making it through another Chicago winter. The crème légère, or light cream, is a mellow vanilla pudding lightened with whipped cream, which is folded into the custard. The peaches are tossed with brown sugar for toasted sweetness, lemon for brightness on the tongue, and mint for depth of flavor. Try fresh basil, lemon balm, or your favorite herb in place of the mint to change things up.

| do-aheads |

*The custard, without the addition of the cream, can be made up to 2 days ahead and kept refrigerated. Rewhisk it before folding in the cream.

**The crème légère can be made up to 24 hours ahead.

for the crème légère

2 cups whole milk

½ vanilla bean, halved lengthwise

6 large egg yolks

⅔ cup sugar

¼ cup cornstarch

1 tablespoon unsalted butter, cold

1 cup heavy cream

for the peaches

4 ripe peaches, pitted and each cut into 6 to 8 wedges

2 teaspoons freshly squeezed lemon juice

¼ cup packed light brown sugar

2 mint leaves, thinly sliced

Have ready near your cooktop a large bowl filled three-quarters full with ice and cover the ice with water.

To make the crème légère, bring the milk and vanilla bean almost to a boil in a large saucepan over medium-high heat. Turn off the heat and let the vanilla steep in the milk for 10 minutes.

In a medium bowl, whisk the egg yolks and sugar until they're light and fluffy. Add the cornstarch and whisk vigorously until no lumps remain. Whisk in $1/4$ cup of the hot milk and then gradually whisk in the remaining hot milk mixture, reserving the saucepan. Strain the mixture through a fine-mesh sieve back into the saucepan. Cook over medium-high heat, whisking constantly, until it thickens and bubbles. Cook and whisk 1 minute more. Remove from the heat and stir in the butter.

Place the pan of custard in the bowl of ice and stir occasionally until thoroughly cooled.*

Meanwhile, whip the cream until it holds stiff peaks. Using a rubber spatula, fold the whipped cream into the cooled custard. Cover with plastic wrap, and refrigerate the crème légère for at least 1 hour.**

For the peaches, place the peach wedges in a bowl and add the lemon juice, brown sugar, and mint. Stir gently, then cover and set aside in the refrigerator for 1 hour.

To serve, place a large spoonful of the crème légère in each of 6 to 8 dessert bowls and put 4 peach wedges in each bowl, arranged alongside the custard. Drizzle the remaining juices from the peaches on top.

mary's **butterballs**

My friend Mary Douglas and her daughter Katie are always cooking and baking delicious things. At the party for Katie's graduation from high school they had a fabulous barbecue (her dad's a great grill master) with quite a spread of desserts. Mary put out an elegant footed glass bowl of these irresistible roly-poly sandwich cookies rolled in sugar (and oh-so-easy too — the dough uses just three ingredients!). I couldn't resist trying the recipe with vanilla sugar for the added warmth and sparkle it brings to your tongue. You can fill these cookies with your favorite jam or make a quick chocolate ganache (3 ounces semi-sweet chocolate melted with ⅓ cup heavy cream; for technique, see Chocolate page 51).

1 cup (2 sticks) unsalted butter, softened

½ cup granulated sugar

1¾ cups all-purpose flour

½ cup raspberry jam or ganache

2 cups vanilla sugar (page 25), for rolling

| do-aheads |

*You can make this dough up to a week in advance and keep it chilled or you can form the balls right after you make the dough and keep them chilled or frozen until you're ready to bake them.

**The cookies can be kept at room temperature for 1 week or frozen, well wrapped, for 1 month.

| you'll need |

2 or 3 cookie sheets

In a mixer fitted with the whisk attachment, beat the butter on medium speed until it's light and fluffy, 3 to 5 minutes. Mix in the granulated sugar and when the mixture is well blended add the flour and mix until it forms a dough. Wrap the dough in plastic and chill for at least 3 hours to make it easier to handle. This also helps prevent the balls from flattening out too much when they're baked.*

Preheat the oven to 375°F.

Taking off pieces of dough with your hands, roll small (3⁄4-inch) balls of dough (about the size of a hazelnut in the shell). Chill them for 30 minutes in the freezer, then place them 2 inches apart on cookie sheets to allow for some spreading. Bake for 10 to 12 minutes, or just until the cookies are firm but not browned. Remove from the oven and let cool on the pans.

Spread the flat face of half of the cooled cookies with the jam or ganache and top with a second cookie to form a little sandwiched ball. The filling will not show very much. Once you've sandwiched them all together, bury them in vanilla sugar to coat the entire outside.**

éclairs with coffee glaze

MAKES 8 TO 10 ÉCLAIRS

One of my great indulgences is pâte à choux, or cream-puff dough, baked and filled with vanilla custard and then dipped in a chewy coffee glaze. Whether they're big or small, piped long for éclairs or round for cream puffs, filled (as they are here) or not (see Chouquettes with Pearl Sugar, page 36), I love them all—which reminds me of a long-told family story. As a six-year-old looking at the pigs at the zoo (my family thought they were ugly, but I didn't), I supposedly said, "If you're going to be an animal lover, you have to love them all!" Well, I am an animal lover *and* a pâte-à-choux lover, too.

To make the filling, bring the milk and vanilla bean almost to a boil in a large saucepan over medium-high heat. Turn off the heat and let steep for 10 minutes.

In a medium bowl, whisk the egg yolks and granulated sugar until they're light and fluffy. Vigorously whisk in the cornstarch until no lumps remain. Whisk in 1/4 cup of the hot milk mixture until it's incorporated. Gradually whisk in the remaining hot milk mixture, reserving the saucepan.

Strain the mixture through a fine-mesh sieve back into the saucepan. Cook over medium-high heat, whisking constantly, until it thickens and bubbles. Cook and whisk for 1 minute more. Remove from the heat and stir in the

do-aheads

*The custard can be made up to 2 days in advance and kept refrigerated.

**The éclairs can be piped out, covered, and frozen up to 2 weeks.

***The glaze can be made up to 4 days in advance and kept at room temperature.

you'll need

Cookie sheet

Parchment paper

Pastry bag with 1 large (1/2-inch) and 1 medium (1/4-inch) plain tip

for the custard filling

2 cups whole milk

1/2 vanilla bean, halved lengthwise

6 large egg yolks

2/3 cup granulated sugar

1/4 cup cornstarch

1 tablespoon unsalted butter, cold

for the éclairs

1 cup plus 1 1/2 teaspoons water

8 tablespoons (1 stick) unsalted butter

1/2 teaspoon salt

1 1/2 teaspoons granulated sugar

1 cup all-purpose flour

4 to 5 large eggs

for the coffee glaze

2 cups powdered sugar

1/4 cup strong coffee or espresso

butter. Scrape into a bowl and press plastic wrap against the surface to prevent a skin from forming. Chill for at least 2 hours before filling and serving the éclairs.*

To make the éclairs, preheat the oven to 425°F. Line a cookie sheet with parchment paper.

In a large saucepan, bring 1 cup water, the butter, salt, and granulated sugar to a boil over medium-high heat, then immediately take the pan off the heat. Stirring with a wooden spoon, add the flour all at once and stir the mixture vigorously until all the flour is incorporated, about 30 seconds. Return the pan to the heat and cook, stirring, for 30 seconds, which allows the mixture to come together and dry out a little more.

Scrape the mixture into a mixer fitted with a paddle attachment. With the mixer on medium speed, blend for 20 seconds to release some of the steam. Add 3 of the eggs, one at a time. Stop mixing after each addition to scrape down the sides of the bowl. Mix until the dough is smooth and glossy and the eggs are completely incorporated. The dough should be thick, but should fall slowly and steadily from the paddle when you lift it out of the bowl. If the dough is still not slowly falling from the paddle, add 1 more egg and mix until it's incorporated.

Using a pastry bag fitted with a large (½-inch) plain tip, pipe 8 to 10 fat lengths of dough (about the size and shape of a jumbo hot dog) onto the prepared cookie sheet, leaving 2 inches of space between them.**

In a small bowl, beat the remaining egg with 1½ teaspoons water. Brush the surface of each éclair with the egg wash. Bake for 15 minutes, then reduce the heat to 375°F and bake until puffed up and light golden brown, about 25 minutes more. Try not to open the oven door too often during the baking or they might deflate. Let cool on the cookie sheet.

Fit a medium (¼-inch) plain pastry tip over your index finger and use it to make a hole in the side of each éclair (or just use your fingertip). Using a pastry bag fitted with a medium plain tip, gently pipe the custard into the éclairs, using only enough to fill them (don't stuff them too full or the filling will ooze back out).

To make the coffee glaze, in a medium bowl whisk the powdered sugar into the coffee until it forms a thick, smooth glaze.***

To serve, dip the tops of the éclairs in the coffee glaze and set them on a cookie sheet. Chill them uncovered for at least 1 hour to set the glaze. Serve chilled.

chouquettes with pearl sugar

Chouquettes are like small cream puffs, but are made with more sugar and a touch of orange flower water. The tops are egg-washed and then sprinkled with a distinctive coarse, opaque white French sugar, sometimes called pearl sugar, before baking (see Sources, Chocolate page 79). They're left unfilled and eaten in France for *quatre heure,* the 4:00 p.m. after-school snack. These are deceptively addictive; it's impossible to eat just one. The recipe comes from Lise, our French nanny from Normandy—the land of butter and cheese.

| do-ahead |
*The dough kisses can be frozen, covered, for up to 2 weeks.

| you'll need |
Parchment paper

Cookie sheet

Pastry bag fitted with a large (½-inch) plain tip

1 cup water

8 tablespoons (1 stick) unsalted butter

3 tablespoons sugar

½ teaspoon salt

½ vanilla bean, halved lengthwise

1 cup all-purpose flour

4 to 5 large eggs

1 teaspoon orange flower water (optional)

Pearl sugar

Preheat the oven to 425°F. Line a cookie sheet with parchment paper.

In a large saucepan, bring 1 cup water, the butter, sugar, salt, and vanilla bean to a boil over medium-high heat. Immediately remove the pan from the heat, and using a wooden spoon, add the flour all at once, stirring vigorously until all the flour is incorporated and absorbed, about 30 seconds. Return the pan to the heat and, continuing to stir, cook until some of the moisture evaporates and the mixture begins to dry out a little, about 30 seconds. Remove the vanilla bean.

Scrape the mixture into the bowl of a mixer fitted with the paddle attachment. Stir on medium speed for 20 seconds or so to allow some of the steam and heat to escape. With the mixer on low add 3 of the eggs, one at a time, stopping after each addition to scrape down the sides of the bowl. Mix until the dough is smooth and glossy and the eggs are completely incorporated. The dough should be thick, but still fall slowly and steadily from the paddle when you lift it out of the bowl. If the dough still clings to the paddle, add 1 more egg and mix until incorporated. Stir in the orange flower water, if using.

Using a pastry bag fitted with a large (1/2-inch) plain tip, pipe 1-inch dough "kisses" spaced 2 inches apart to allow for expansion onto the prepared cookie sheet.*

In a small bowl, beat the remaining egg with 1 1/2 teaspoons water. Brush the tops of the dough with the egg wash and sprinkle with the pearl sugar.

Bake for 15 minutes, then reduce the heat to 375°F and bake until the chouquettes are puffed up, light golden brown, and have no more yellow pastry color showing through, about 20 minutes more. (Try not to open the oven door because a decrease in oven heat will cause the chouquettes to deflate.) Remove from the oven and let cool on the cookie sheet.

vanilla-scented peach

tarte tatin

MAKES ONE 9-INCH TART, OR 8 SERVINGS

When I was at Bernachon, the best pastry shop in Lyon, France, the owner, Maurice Bernachon, taught me many things but one of the things I remember most is "show your best side," which in the pastry kitchen means that you should show off your ingredients, especially the pricey ones. Here, the vanilla bean that perfumes the tart is lying on the top of the tart when the dessert is turned out onto a platter for serving. I'm not sure, but I think this might be my favorite dessert. Don't tell anyone.

Mexican vanilla beans, with their slightly spicy overtones, work well here, though mellow Madagascar Bourbon beans are good too. And long gone are the days when I make puff pastry from scratch because now I can find several quality brands at my local market; look for one made with all butter.

1 sheet store-bought frozen puff pastry, thawed overnight in the refrigerator

8 tablespoons (1 stick) unsalted butter

1 cup sugar

1 vanilla bean, halved lengthwise

1 cinnamon stick

1 tablespoon freshly squeezed lemon juice

2 tablespoons vanilla brandy (see page 20)

8 ripe peaches, halved and pitted

| do-ahead |

*You can cut the puff pastry round and refrigerate, covered with plastic wrap, up to a day ahead.

| you'll need |

Cookie sheet

9-inch round cake pan or ovenproof sauté pan

Rimmed platter or plate

Cut a 10-inch round disk out of the puff pastry, prick it all over with the tines of a fork, and put on a cookie sheet in the refrigerator to keep cold.*

Preheat the oven to 425°F.

Put the butter in a heavy, round 9-inch cake pan or ovenproof 9-inch sauté pan, and melt it over medium heat until it's bubbling slightly. Add the sugar and stir with a wooden spoon until combined. Add the vanilla bean and cinnamon stick and stir to help release the seeds. Continue cooking the caramel, stirring occasionally until it's light amber, 3 to 5 minutes. Carefully add the lemon juice and brandy—the mixture will spatter—and stir, cooking until the caramel has smoothed out, another minute or so.

Remove the pan from the heat and, using tongs, arrange the vanilla bean and cinnamon stick in the middle of the pan. Place the peach halves cut-side up in two concentric rings around the pan, packing them tightly so that they overlap, ending with one half in the middle. Return the pan to the heat and bring the caramel to a boil. Remove from the heat and place the puff pastry disk over the fruit, leaving any overhang as the crust will shrink.

Bake the tart until the pastry is puffed and golden, about 25 minutes. Remove from the oven and let cool in the pan, 45 minutes to 1 hour.

Place a rimmed platter or plate over the tart and invert to turn the tart out of the pan. If it sticks, put the pan on the stove to heat it briefly, so that the tart will drop out when inverted. Serve it whole on the platter, then cut the tart into wedges, removing the vanilla bean and cinnamon stick.

vanilla **charlotte**

MAKES ONE 8-INCH CHARLOTTE,
OR 6 TO 8 SERVINGS

No one makes charlottes anymore, which means they're destined for a comeback. A charlotte is a dessert formed in a high, straight-walled mold lined with ladyfingers, cake, or sliced bread and filled with either cooked fruit, such as apples, or a vanilla Bavarian cream like the one I'm using here. Made in one large mold (you can find charlotte molds in good cookware shops), it's a regal-looking dessert that makes an unusual yet light ending for a special occasion.

If you have a charlotte mold you do not need to line it. Otherwise, line an 8-inch springform pan or soufflé dish with parchment paper using a circle for the bottom and a strip 4 inches wide around the sides. Dab a little softened butter or a spritz of nonstick cooking spray in the pan to anchor the paper. Generously spray or grease the parchment or charlotte mold. Stand the ladyfingers up around the insides of the pan.

Pick over the raspberries, setting aside the best ones, a little less than ½ pint, to make a circle around the edge of the finished charlotte.

do-ahead
*The charlotte will keep in the refrigerator for up to 3 days.

you'll need
Charlotte mold, 8-inch springform pan, or soufflé dish
Parchment paper
Instant-read thermometer, optional

1 recipe ladyfingers (page 44) or 1 (7-ounce) package store-bought
2 (½-pint) containers raspberries
4 cups whole milk
1 vanilla bean, halved lengthwise
1 tablespoon powdered gelatin
2 tablespoons cold water
12 large egg yolks
1⅓ cups granulated sugar
White chocolate curls (see Chocolate page 20)
Powdered sugar

Have ready near your cooktop a large bowl. Fill the bowl three-quarters full with ice and cover the ice with water.

Bring the milk and vanilla bean to a boil in a large saucepan over medium-high heat. As soon as it comes to a boil, turn off the heat and let the vanilla steep in the milk for 10 minutes.

Gradually sprinkle the gelatin over the cold water in a small bowl and set aside for the gelatin to soften.

In a medium bowl, whisk the egg yolks with the granulated sugar for about 1 minute to combine and then gradually pour in the hot milk, whisking continuously. Return the mixture to the saucepan and, stirring constantly with a wooden spoon, cook over medium heat until the sauce has thickened and is 180°F on an instant-read thermometer, being careful not to overcook it or it will break. (If you don't have a thermometer, test the mixture by dipping a wooden spoon into it, and then running your finger down the back of the spoon. If the stripe remains intact, the mixture is ready; if the edges blur, the mixture is not cooked enough yet.)

Immediately stir the softened gelatin into the custard until it's dissolved and then strain the mixture through a fine-mesh sieve into a medium bowl. Put the bowl of custard into the bowl of ice water and stir frequently until the custard starts to cool and thicken.

Fold in the less-than-perfect berries (don't worry if the berries break up a bit) and then pour the custard into the pan lined with the ladyfingers. Spread the top of the custard to smooth it. Cover the charlotte with plastic wrap and put in the refrigerator to chill for at least 4 hours.*

To serve, trim the ladyfingers even with the top of the custard. Put a serving platter upside down over the pan and quickly invert it. Remove the mold and parchment. Arrange the reserved raspberries around the edge of the charlotte and pile white chocolate curls in the center. Dust with powdered sugar and cut into wedges for serving.

vanilla **malteds**

MAKES 4 SERVINGS

When I was a kid our big weekend event was staying home on Saturday night and watching a horror movie. My dad, Bob, would make his stellar popcorn and my mom, Myrna, would make frosty thick malteds in the blender we got with S & H Green Stamps (we would get these for grocery purchases and paste them in books to be redeemed for merchandise). Malted milk powder (I use Carnation brand) is a perfect part-ner to vanilla and you can usually find it in the grocery aisle with the ice cream cone and sundae supplies. You could make this more exotic by flavoring it with ginger powder, raspberry jam, fresh blueberries, or go—bananas!

Combine the vanilla ice cream, half-and-half, malted milk powder, and vanilla extract in a blender and process until the mixture is thick and creamy. Pour into tall glasses and serve with elbow straws.

1 pint good-quality vanilla ice cream
1 cup half-and-half
3 tablespoons malted milk powder
1 teaspoon pure vanilla extract

vanilla **butter caramels**

MAKES 64 PIECES

When my husband and I take driving trips with our kids through Illinois and our neighboring states of Wisconsin, Indiana, and Michigan, we love stopping at roadside stands along the way to pick up delicious ripe, local fruit. If we're lucky there are some home-baked pies as well, but what I always keep an eye out for are homemade caramels, wrapped in wax paper with twisted ends, usually on display next to the cash register. This vanilla version was inspired by those treats.

Line an 8 by 8-inch pan, preferably one with straight sides and square corners, with aluminum foil and grease the foil well.

Put the sugar in a heavy medium saucepan. Slowly add the water by pouring it around the inside wall of the pan to avoid splashing any sugar crystals onto the sides of the saucepan. Let the water soak into the sugar completely.

Bring the water and sugar to a boil over high heat and continue cooking until the liquid is golden. Turn off the heat and, with a wooden spoon, carefully stir in the butter and then the vanilla and cream. Pour into the prepared pan and let cool until firmly set, anywhere from 1 to 2 hours.

Cut into 1-inch squares and wrap each one in decorative cellophane or wax paper.*

| do-ahead |
*These caramels keep well for 2 weeks stored at room temperature.

| you'll need |
8-inch square pan, preferably one with straight sides and square corners
Aluminum foil
Cellophane or wax paper

5 cups sugar
1 cup water
6 tablespoons (3/4 stick) unsalted butter
1 teaspoon pure vanilla extract
1 cup heavy cream

ladyfingers with strawberries and cream

MAKES 8 SERVINGS

We used to buy ladyfingers—long finger-shaped crisp vanilla-flavored biscuits—by the case at one of my former restaurants for our tiramisù. But if I have the time I really prefer to make my own; they're actually quite simple and nothing beats homemade ladyfingers served with ripe berries and whipped cream. Freshly whipped cream is wonderful, of course, but for convenience, sometimes I use canned real whipped cream. (There are many good brands on the market now made with organic milk and without stabilizers.) This makes a nice light and fun dessert that's like strawberry shortcake in one bite.

| do-ahead |

*Ladyfingers keep in an airtight container at room temperature for up to 4 days.

| you'll need |

Parchment paper
Cookie sheet
Large pastry bag fitted with a large (1/2-inch) plain tip

for the ladyfingers

5 large eggs, separated
1/4 cup granulated sugar
1 teaspoon pure vanilla extract
1 cup powdered sugar, plus extra for dusting the ladyfingers
1 scant cup cake flour

1 cup heavy cream
2 tablespoons granulated sugar
1 pint strawberries, washed

On a piece of parchment paper, draw 2 parallel lines 4 inches apart to use as a guide for piping the ladyfingers. Draw a second set of lines 1½ inches from the first set. Turn the paper over and place pencil-side down on a cookie sheet.

Preheat the oven to 375°F. Have a large pastry bag fitted with a large (½-inch) plain tip ready.

To make the ladyfingers, in a mixer fitted with the whisk attachment, whip the egg yolks and granulated sugar on medium speed until the mixture is light and thickened and falls back in a ribbon when the whisk is lifted from the batter, about 5 minutes. Stir in the vanilla.

In another clean, dry bowl, whip the egg whites on low speed until they're foamy, then increase the speed to medium and whip while adding the powdered sugar gradually. Increase the speed to high and whip until the whites hold a stiff peak.

Sift half of the flour over the yolks and fold in the flour using a rubber spatula. Fold the whipped whites into the yolks and then sift and fold in the remaining flour.

Fill the pastry bag with the batter and pipe finger-thick stripes 1½ inches apart between the sets of parallel lines.

Sift powdered sugar heavily over the tops of the ladyfingers.

Bake until golden brown, 8 to 10 minutes. Let the ladyfingers cool on the cookie sheet before lifting them off the parchment paper.*

Whip the cream with the 2 tablespoons granulated sugar until the cream holds medium peaks.

Serve 2 to 3 ladyfingers on dessert plates with a small bowl of whipped cream and whole strawberries to dip into the cream.

lisa's **almond macaroons**

MAKES 2 DOZEN MACAROONS

My pastry sous-chef at Tru, Lisa Mortimer, makes these for our restaurant staff's "family meal." They're so irresistible that it's hard not to eat them until we get sick. They're chewy, moist, vanilla-y, and so easy to make.

Preheat the oven to 375°F. Have ready a pastry bag fitted with a large (½-inch) plain tip and a cookie sheet lined with parchment paper.

In a mixer fitted with the paddle attachment, beat the almond paste with the powdered sugar on low speed until smooth. Add the vanilla and then the egg whites, and mix until the mixture becomes a smooth batter.*

Fill the pastry bag with the batter and pipe 1¼-inch-diameter disks (about the size of a half dollar) about 1-inch apart onto the prepared cookie sheet.

Bake for 15 to 20 minutes, or until the macaroons are golden brown. Remove from the oven and let them cool on the cookie sheet.

Using a fork, drizzle the chocolate over the macaroons and allow to set up.**

| **do-aheads** |

*The batter can be made up to 2 days ahead before baking and kept in the refrigerator or frozen in a sealed plastic bag for up to 1 month.

**The macaroons keep in an airtight tin for 1 week.

| **you'll need** |

Pastry bag with a large (½-inch) plain tip
Cookie sheet
Parchment paper

8 ounces almond paste, cut into large pieces

2 cups powdered sugar

½ teaspoon pure vanilla extract

¼ cup egg whites (from 2 to 3 large eggs)

4 ounces semi-sweet chocolate, melted (optional)

vita's **ricotta doughnuts**

MAKES 16 DOUGHNUTS

My Sicilian-American mother-in-law, Vita Seidita, taught me how to make these tender-on-the-inside, crisp-on-the-outside doughnuts, which she often made for her family on Sunday mornings. All the kids would hover near the stove as she lifted the hot doughnuts out of the oil onto a brown paper bag for draining, and then their job was to roll them quickly in cinnamon sugar. Cinnamon sugar is 1 teaspoon cinnamon combined with 1/3 cup sugar (you can double or triple this and keep some in your pantry for whenever). For a more traditional doughnut taste, along with the vanilla, add a pinch of nutmeg to the batter.

In a large bowl, stir together the eggs, granulated sugar, ricotta, flour, baking powder, and vanilla until combined, being careful not to overmix the batter.*

In a deep, heavy pot fitted with a deep-frying thermometer, heat 2 to 3 inches of oil to 325°F. Drop the batter by small ice cream scoopfuls or small spoonfuls (use 2 teaspoons) into the oil and fry for 3 minutes, turning often, until golden brown on each side. You may need to fry the doughnuts in two batches to avoid crowding the pot. Break open a doughnut to make sure it's cooked all the way through. Scoop out the doughnuts with a slotted spoon and transfer to paper towels or a brown paper bag to drain. Let the oil come back up to temperature and repeat with the remaining batter.

Dust the doughnuts with or roll them in powdered sugar or cinnamon sugar and serve hot.

| do-ahead |
*You can cover the bowl of batter and put it in the refrigerator at this point (up to 1 day ahead) until you're ready to fry, but you might have to increase the frying time slightly to compensate for the colder batter.

| you'll need |
Deep-frying thermometer

6 large eggs

1/2 cup granulated sugar

1 pound whole- or skim-milk ricotta cheese

2 1/2 cups all-purpose flour

1 heaping tablespoon baking powder

1 teaspoon pure vanilla extract

Canola or vegetable oil, for frying

Powdered sugar or cinnamon sugar (optional, see head note)

mini **black-and-whites**

Black-and-whites are one of the great New York bakery traditions: a perfect vanilla and lemon-scented cakey cookie—made with cake flour—frosted on one half with chocolate glaze and the other half with vanilla glaze. It's basically a cookie for people who hate choosing between flavors. Here's a mini version that is cuter and easier for dunking.

| do-aheads |

*The dough can be formed and frozen, well wrapped, for up to one month.

**The balls of dough can be refrigerated up to 2 days.

***The cookies can be kept in an airtight tin at room temperature for 3 days.

| you'll need |

2 to 3 cookie sheets

Parchment paper

for the cookies

8 tablespoons (1 stick) unsalted butter, softened

1 cup granulated sugar

2 large eggs

1/2 cup whole milk

1/4 teaspoon pure vanilla extract

1/8 teaspoon pure lemon extract

1 1/4 cups cake flour

1 1/4 cups all-purpose flour

1/2 teaspoon baking powder

1/4 teaspoon salt

for the icing

2 cups powdered sugar

5 tablespoons milk

1 teaspoon pure vanilla extract

2 tablespoons cocoa powder, preferably Dutch-processed

To make the cookies, line 2 or 3 cookie sheets with parchment paper.

Using a mixer fitted with the paddle attachment, beat the butter on medium speed until light in color, then add the granulated sugar and beat until fluffy, 3 to 5 minutes. Beat in the eggs, milk, and vanilla and lemon extracts.

In a large bowl, stir together both of the flours, the baking powder, and salt and then add to the sugar–egg mixture, mixing until thoroughly combined.*

Using a small ice cream scoop, make 1-inch balls of dough. Space them evenly on the cookie sheets and chill in the refrigerator for at least 1 hour.**

Preheat the oven to 375°F.

Wrap a flat-bottomed mug or drinking glass with plastic wrap. Press down on each ball of dough to flatten it into a disk about 1/4 inch thick and 1 1/4 inches in diameter. Bake for 15 minutes, or until golden. Transfer to a cooling rack and let cool.

To make the vanilla icing, in a medium bowl stir the powdered sugar with 3 tablespoons of the milk and the vanilla until smooth. To make the chocolate icing, transfer half of the vanilla icing to another bowl and stir in the cocoa powder and remaining 2 tablespoons milk.

When the cookies have cooled, turn them over so the flat sides face up. Using a small spatula or a butter knife, spread vanilla icing on half of the flat surface of each cookie, then spread the other half with chocolate icing. Let the icing set for 30 minutes.***

vanilla-blueberry **crumb cake**

MAKES ONE 9-INCH SQUARE CAKE, OR 8 SERVINGS

My husband, Jimmy, has been going to bakeries and collecting their business cards as a hobby since way before I married him. That's part of *why* I married him. He's always told me about his favorite childhood bakery back in East Islip, Long Island, called Stanley's: The apple turnovers and golden crumb cake were his favorites. I created this moist vanilla cake with its crumbly topping to bring back memories for him. Besides, I thought, what better way to use some of the twenty pounds of blueberries we pick every August? In the fall I make the cake with chopped fresh cranberries and it might be even better . . . but I can't decide.

| do-ahead |
*The cake can be kept at room temperature, covered, for up to 3 days.

| you'll need |
9-inch square cake pan

2 cups all-purpose flour
1 cup granulated sugar
$\frac{1}{2}$ cup packed light brown sugar
1 cup (2 sticks) unsalted butter
1 cup sour cream
1 large egg
1 teaspoon pure vanilla extract
1 teaspoon baking powder
1 teaspoon baking soda
$\frac{1}{2}$ teaspoon salt
1 pint blueberries

Preheat the oven to 350°F. Butter and flour a 9-inch square cake pan or line it with parchment paper and set it aside.

In a mixer fitted with the paddle attachment, combine 1½ cups of the flour, the granulated sugar, brown sugar, and butter on low speed until the mixture is blended and starts to form clumps. Set aside 1 cup of the mixture to use for the crumb topping.

In a small bowl, whisk together the sour cream, egg, vanilla, baking powder, baking soda, and salt until combined. Stir in the remaining ½ cup flour, then scrape this mixture into the mixer and beat on medium speed until it forms a smooth batter. Spread it into the prepared cake pan. Sprinkle the blueberries over the batter, press them down a little, and then sprinkle with the reserved crumb topping.

Bake for 40 minutes, or until the cake is firm to the touch and a skewer or toothpick inserted into the center comes out clean. Let the cake cool in the pan set on a cooling rack.*

Cut into 8 rectangles just before serving.

lemon-vanilla **pound cake**

MAKES ONE 10-INCH TUBE OR BUNDT CAKE,
OR 8 TO 10 SERVINGS

The best pound cake I've ever had is my mother-in-law's and she got the recipe from her neighbor, who told her never to give it out to anyone (particularly "my kind," a pastry chef/ author who publishes and teaches on TV). I've reworked it slightly to give it a more puckery lemon flavor by brushing the finished cake with lemon syrup. I also like to bake it in a sunflower pan for my niece Gemma. In our family we call it *girosole*, which is Italian for sunflower, Gemma's favorite.

| do-ahead |
*The cake can be made up to 2 days ahead.

| you'll need |
12-cup or 10-inch tube pan or decorative Bundt pan
Pastry brush

12 tablespoons (1½ sticks) unsalted butter
1 cup whole milk
4 large eggs
2¼ cups sugar
2 teaspoons pure vanilla extract
1 teaspoon lemon extract
Grated zest of 1 lemon
2 cups all-purpose flour
2 teaspoons baking powder
Juice of 1 lemon

Melt 4 tablespoons of the butter. Generously brush a 10-inch tube pan or decorative Bundt pan with the melted butter and refrigerate it for a few minutes. Once the butter has hardened, brush it again to cover any spots you missed the first time. Set the pan aside.

Preheat the oven to 350°F.

Bring the milk and remaining 8 tablespoons of butter just to a boil in a medium saucepan. Set aside.

In an electric mixer fitted with the whisk attachment, whip the eggs on medium-high speed until light and very fluffy, 5 to 7 minutes. Reduce the speed to medium and stir in 2 cups of the sugar, the vanilla and lemon extracts, and lemon zest. On low speed, gradually mix in the flour. Pour in the hot milk mixture, then add the baking powder, and stir until the batter is thoroughly combined. Pour the batter into the buttered pan and bake for 50 to 60 minutes, or until a skewer inserted in the center comes out clean.

While the cake is baking, blend the lemon juice with the remaining 1/4 cup sugar in a small bowl and set aside.

Remove the cake from the oven and let it cool in the pan for 5 minutes. Invert the cake onto a cooling rack. Place the rack over a rimmed baking sheet and brush the warm cake all over with the lemon syrup, letting the syrup soak in as you go. Wrap the cake in plastic wrap and set aside at room temperature.*

individual lemon-vanilla
pudding cakes

MAKES 8 TO 12 SERVINGS (DEPENDING ON THE SIZE OF THE
RAMEKINS OR BAKING CUPS)

Pudding cakes fascinate me. Once the batter hits the oven it begins to separate into layers: a bottom layer of pudding with a layer of sponge cake on top. To quote Larry David, "It's like a delicious sponge." I love these refreshing vanilla and citrus versions which are miraculously light. I'd suggest serving them with a small scoop of raspberry sorbet on top.

| do-ahead |
*The pudding cakes can be made up to 6 hours ahead of serving and served at room temperature.

| you'll need |
Eight 4- to 6-ounce ramekins
Baking dish large enough to hold the ramekins
Aluminum foil

8 tablespoons (1 stick) unsalted butter, softened

1/3 cup plus 3/4 cup sugar

5 large eggs, separated

1/4 cup plus 2 tablespoons all-purpose flour

1 1/4 cups whole milk

Grated zest of 2 lemons

2/3 cup freshly squeezed lemon juice

1 teaspoon pure vanilla extract

Preheat the oven to 325°F. Brush eight 4- to 6-ounce ramekins or custard cups with 3 tablespoons of the butter and place them in a large baking dish. Bring a tea kettle or medium saucepan of water to a boil.

In a mixer fitted with the paddle attachment, beat the remaining 5 tablespoons butter with ⅓ cup of the sugar until it's light and fluffy. One at a time mix in the egg yolks and then fold in the flour. Don't worry if the mixture separates. On low speed stir in the milk, lemon zest, lemon juice, and vanilla until combined.

In a mixer fitted with the whisk attachment (and in a dry, clean bowl), whip the egg whites on medium speed until they're foamy. Gradually add the remaining ¾ cup sugar, whipping on medium speed until the whites are glossy and stiff but not dry. Using a rubber spatula, stir a large spoonful of the whites into the lemon mixture just to lighten it and then fold in the rest of the whites.

Divide the batter among the prepared ramekins, filling them three-quarters full. Pour boiling water in the baking dish to come halfway up the sides of the ramekins. Cover the baking dish with aluminum foil and bake the puddings for 30 minutes, or until puffed and set.

Remove the puddings from the oven, uncover, and let cool for 10 minutes before serving.*

boston cream **cupcakes**

What could be better than your own individual golden cake filled with vanilla custard and covered with a chewy chocolate glaze? I like making these for two reasons: First, they're a perfect combination of chocolate and vanilla in an individual portion (a little more vanilla than chocolate), and second, they're one of my restaurant partner Rich Melman's favorite desserts.

for the cupcakes

8 tablespoons (1 stick) unsalted butter, softened

1 cup sugar

1/2 teaspoon pure vanilla extract

2 large eggs

1 1/2 cups sifted cake flour

1 1/2 teaspoons baking powder

1/4 teaspoon salt

1/2 cup whole milk

1/2 recipe éclair custard filling (page 34)*

for the chocolate glaze

1 cup heavy cream

8 ounces semi-sweet chocolate, chopped

| do-aheads |

*The custard can be made and refrigerated up to 2 days in advance.

**The cupcakes can be made 2 days ahead, wrapped well, and refrigerated or frozen for 2 months.

***The glaze can be made a week in advance and refrigerated. The glaze can be reheated over a pan of simmering water or in the microwave.

| you'll need |

12-cup muffin tin

Paper cupcake liners

Pastry bag with a large (1/2-inch) plain tip, optional

Preheat the oven to 350°F. Line a 12-cup muffin tin with paper cupcake liners.

In a mixer fitted with the whisk attachment, beat the butter on medium speed until light and fluffy, 3 to 5 minutes. Add the sugar and continue to whip. Add the vanilla and gradually mix in the eggs, one by one, until well combined. Sift together the flour, baking powder, and salt. Add the dry ingredients to the butter mixture in 3 batches, alternating with the milk and ending with the dry ingredients.

Pour the batter into the prepared pan, filling each slot three-quarters full. Bake for 20 to 25 minutes, until the cupcakes are puffed, firm in the center, and light golden brown on top. Let cool in the pan on a cooling rack.**

To fill the cupcakes, use a small paring knife to remove a plug of cake from the top center of each cake and set the plugs aside. With a pastry bag fitted with a large ($\frac{1}{2}$-inch) plain tip, pipe or spoon the custard into the cavities. Trim each plug so that it is a flat coin. Top the filled cupcake cavities with the coins and chill for 30 minutes while you make the glaze.

To make the chocolate glaze, heat the cream in a saucepan or in the microwave until almost boiling. Meanwhile place the chocolate in a medium bowl. Pour the hot cream over the chopped chocolate and whisk until melted.***

Dip the chilled cupcakes in the warm chocolate glaze to coat the top. Refrigerate until serving.

golden **vanilla layer cake** with
chocolate fudge frosting

MAKES ONE 9-INCH CAKE, OR 12 TO 16 SERVINGS

This cake is the one Gio and I make on Father's Day to satisfy all the father and grandfather figures in his life. It's a classic with coffee and tastes good the next day, too. I just think seeing an old-fashioned layer cake sitting on the kitchen counter for a few days is one of the most comforting sights ever. It makes me feel like all is right with the world.

| do-aheads |

*The unfrosted cakes can be wrapped in plastic and kept at room temperature for 1 day, in the refrigerator for up to 4 days, or frozen for 2 weeks. Defrost on the counter overnight.

**The frosting keeps well in the fridge for 2 weeks.

***The frosted cake can be kept at room temperature for 3 to 4 days. Cover with an inverted bowl if you do not have a cake plate with a cover.

| you'll need |

Two 9-inch round cake pans
Parchment paper

for the cake

3 cups sifted cake flour

1 tablespoon baking powder

1/2 teaspoon salt

1 cup (2 sticks) unsalted butter, softened

2 cups granulated sugar

4 large eggs

1 teaspoon pure vanilla extract

1 teaspoon almond extract

1 cup whole milk

for the frosting

6 tablespoons (3/4 stick) unsalted butter, softened

3 cups powdered sugar

3 ounces unsweetened chocolate, melted

1 1/2 teaspoons pure vanilla extract

3 tablespoons milk

Preheat the oven to 375°F. Butter and flour the walls of two 9-inch round cake pans and then line each pan with a circle of parchment paper.

To make the cake, sift the flour, baking powder, and salt together 3 times into a bowl or onto a piece of parchment and set aside.

In a mixer fitted with the whisk attachment, beat the butter on medium speed until it's light and fluffy, 3 to 5 minutes. Add the granulated sugar and whip until it's blended. One at a time, add the eggs, mixing after each addition until well combined. Whip in the vanilla and almond extracts. With the mixer on low speed, add the flour mixture to the butter mixture in thirds, alternating with the milk and ending with the flour. Mix until just combined after each addition.

Pour the batter into the prepared cake pans and bake until the cakes are golden and firm to the touch, 25 to 30 minutes. Remove from the oven and let cool in the pans.*

Meanwhile make the frosting. In a mixer fitted with the whisk attachment, whip the butter on medium speed until it's light and fluffy, 3 to 5 minutes. With the mixer on low speed, add the powdered sugar gradually. Mix in the melted chocolate, then the vanilla. Add the milk by spoonfuls until the frosting is spreadable but still thick and fudgy.**

Remove the parchment from one of the cake layers and place the cake on a serving platter. Using an offset or small icing spatula, spread the top with some frosting. Place the second cake layer on the first, bottom-side up so the cake has a nice flat top. Remove the parchment and press down lightly to secure the layers. Frost the top and sides of the cake.***

To serve, cut into wedges.

baked **ricotta custards** with
raspberry mint salad

MAKES 10 TO 12 SERVINGS

My New York pastry chef friend Richard Leach shared this recipe with me and I absolutely love it. Whether topped with fruit or caramelized like a crème brûlée, it's simple and delicious, reminiscent of Italian-style ricotta cheesecake, only lighter. It's also what I serve friends and family who request a sugar-free dessert (by just substituting an equal amount of Splenda for the sugar).

| do-aheads |
*The custards can be kept, covered, in the refrigerator for up to 3 days before serving.

**The raspberry mint salad can be refrigerated for up to 8 hours before serving.

| you'll need |
Ten to twelve 4-ounce ramekins or custard cups
Large baking dish or roasting pan

for the custard
10 ounces cream cheese, at room temperature
1 cup whole-milk ricotta cheese
2 large eggs
1 large egg white
½ teaspoon pure vanilla extract
½ cup sugar
½ cup heavy cream

for the raspberry mint salad
2 (½-pint) containers of raspberries
2 tablespoons sugar
2 mint leaves, thinly sliced

Preheat the oven to 250°F. Bring a tea kettle or medium saucepan of water to a boil. Have ready ten to twelve 4-ounce ramekins in a baking dish or roasting pan that's large enough to hold them all.

To make the custard, using an electric mixer fitted with the whisk attachment, beat the cream cheese on medium speed until it's light, smooth, and fluffy, 5 to 7 minutes. Add the ricotta and mix until combined. Mix in the eggs and egg white one at a time until combined, then mix in the vanilla, sugar, and cream.

Pour the batter into the ramekins, filling almost full, and pour the boiling water around them to come halfway up the sides. Bake for 45 minutes, or until the custards are set but not colored. Remove from the oven and let cool in the water bath to room temperature. Remove from the water, cover, and put in the refrigerator to chill for at least 1 hour.*

For the raspberry mint salad, using a fork, mash a quarter of the berries in a bowl with the sugar until puréed. Fold in the whole berries along with the mint.**

To serve, spoon the raspberry mint salad over the top of the chilled custards.

dessert **french toast**

MAKES 4 SERVINGS

As a chef, I rarely have time for breakfast in the morning. Maybe that's why I crave things like bacon and eggs, even for dinner. Here's yet another attempt to satisfy both my love of vanilla as well as my yearning for breakfast, all in one meal.

3 large eggs

$\frac{1}{2}$ cup sugar

Pinch of salt

$\frac{1}{2}$ teaspoon pure vanilla extract

1 cup half-and-half

1 cup whole milk

4 thick slices brioche or challah

1 pink grapefruit

$\frac{1}{2}$ cup pure maple syrup

4 tablespoons ($\frac{1}{2}$ stick) unsalted butter, melted

$\frac{1}{2}$ cup mascarpone, at room temperature

| do-aheads |

*You can refrigerate the custard overnight in a covered container.

**The grapefruit can be sectioned and kept in the refrigerator overnight.

| you'll need |

12 by 17-inch rimmed baking sheet or shallow baking dish

Pancake griddle, grill pan, or large sauté pan

In a medium bowl, whisk the eggs to break them up, then stir in the sugar, salt, and vanilla. Gradually whisk in the half-and-half and milk. Pour the mixture into a rimmed baking sheet or shallow baking dish.* Put as many bread slices in the pan as will fit, and soak the bread slices, turning to soak both sides. Set aside. Repeat with any remaining bread.

Using a small, sharp knife, peel the grapefruit and then cut between the membranes to free the grapefruit sections.**

Put the maple syrup in a medium sauté pan and bring it to a boil over medium heat. Add the grapefruit sections and let cook on one side for 30 seconds, then turn them to cook on the other side for 30 seconds. Remove from the heat and set aside.

Preheat a griddle to medium-low or heat a grill pan or sauté pan over medium-low heat. Brush with the butter. Cook the soaked bread slices on the griddle or in the pan for 3 to 5 minutes on each side, until golden brown.

To serve, spoon the grapefruit and syrup over the French toast and serve topped with a dollop of mascarpone.

vanilla and orange-scented
caramel sauce

MAKES ABOUT 1½ CUPS

I'm always happy when I know that I have some of this sauce on
a shelf in my fridge. With its subtle hint of lemon it's yummy on
vanilla ice cream and can be served as a dipping sauce for fresh
fruit. Try it also with Chocolate Waffles (Chocolate page 51).

Heat the cream with the orange zest in a small saucepan
over medium-high heat until it comes almost to a boil. Set
aside to infuse the cream with the orange.

Put the sugar in a medium high-walled saucepan (this will
help protect you from the bubbling hot caramel) and pour
the water down the walls of the pan. Draw your finger twice
through the center of the sugar to make an "x" just to moisten the sugar. Bring the mixture to a boil. Cook without stirring, swirling the pan occasionally, until the sugar turns
golden amber, 5 to 10 minutes.

Immediately remove from the heat and, using a wooden
spoon, *carefully* stir in the infused orange cream; the hot
caramel will spatter a little at first. Add the vanilla and strain
through a fine-mesh sieve. Serve warm or transfer to a container and chill in the refrigerator until ready to serve.*

| **do-ahead** |
*The sauce can be kept in the refrigerator
for 1 week and served cold or reheated
and served warm.

²/₃ cup heavy cream
Zest from ½ orange removed in
    ½-inch strips with a peeler
1¼ cups sugar
⅓ cup water
½ teaspoon pure vanilla extract

**vita's ricotta doughnuts,
page 47**

**vanilla charlotte,
page 40**

vanilla-blueberry crumb cake,
page 50

chouquettes with pearl sugar, page 36

vanilla-scented peach tarte tatin,
page 38

vanilla raspberry rice pudding with lemon vanilla caramel,
page 26

mary's butterballs,
page 32

**frozen poppy-seed mousse with vanilla-poached stone fruit,
page 20**

individual chocolate pavlova,
page 64

peanut butter cocoa crisp treats,
page 59

chocolate-praline cake in a jar,
page 40

heart throbs with marshmallow filling,
page 47

chocolate-almond upside-down cake, page 38

chocolate fudge soccer cakes,
page 42

mocha panna cotta,
page 28

deep chocolate shortbread,
page 26

Acknowledgments

Thank you to my friends, family, and colleagues, especially Jane Dystel; Lisa Weiss; Jeff Kauck; Rica Allannic; Pam Krauss; my husband, Jimmy Seidita; my dad, Bob Gand; Rick Tramonto; Lana Rae; Ina Pinkney, the Breakfast Queen (oh those heavenly hots of yours!); Rich Melman; Judy Anderson and family; Marthe Young and family; my assistant Jeffrey Ward; Karen and Ron Filbert, who bottle my Gale's Root Beer for me; Caroline Myss; our doulas, Meridith Wu and Jackie Foreman; Roxana and Flora Nemens; Gio's fourth-grade teacher Ms. Susan McMillan; Michelle Marino at Bakeworks, who makes my Gale At Home bakeware; and the Food Network.

And thank you to the friends and family who inspired me and shared their recipes with me for this book, especially my late (in both senses of the word) mother, Myrna Gand; Grandma Elsie Grossman; Greta and Robert Pearson; my mother-in-law, Vita Seidita; Karen Katz and family; my pastry sous chef Lisa Mortimer; the Shay family; our au pair, Lise Hebert; Gio's third-grade teachers, Mr. Jackson and Mr. Shields; Mary and Katie Douglas; Elizabeth Kisch; and Richard Leach.

Sources

Chefshop.com
877-337-2491
www.chefshop.com
Large selection of food products, including specialty chocolates and vanilla

Chocosphere
877-992-4626
www.chocosphere.com
All kinds of premium chocolate, including Valrhona

King Arthur Flour Company and Baker's Catalogue
800-827-6836
www.kingarthurflour.com
Extensive selection of equipment such as Twinkie-style pans and madeleine molds, plus baking ingredients, including pearl sugar, specialty flours, specialty cocoa powder, and vanillas

Nielsen-Massey
800-525-7873
www.nielsenmassey.com
Manufacturers of pure vanilla extract, powders, and pastes

Penzeys Spices
800-741-7787
www.penzeys.com
Very extensive selection of international spices, including Mexican cinnamon (called *canela*), and vanilla beans

The Spice House
312-274-0378
www.thespicehouse.com
Another very extensive selection of spices and vanillas; the staff is very helpful if you phone

Sur La Table
800-243-0582
www.surlatable.com
Excellent equipment for the home baker: madeleine molds, parchment paper, cake pans plus quality ingredients

The Vanilla Company
800-757-7511
www.vanilla.com
This is *the* website for vanilla lovers. In addition to information about the vanilla orchid they sell beans and extracts

Williams-Sonoma
800-541-2233
www.williamsonoma.com
Online and mail-order catalogs for equipment and ingredients

Zingerman's
888-636-8162
www.zingermans.com
Great selection of specialty chocolates and vanillas

Bake for 12 to 15 minutes, or until the phyllo is crispy and you can see it's starting to brown (look at the corners where the cocoa coating is thinned). Remove the pans from the oven and let cool, leaving the weighting pan on top. When cool remove the weighting pan and parchment and break the phyllo into free-form pieces roughly 3 inches square. You will need 12 pieces for this dessert. Store in an airtight container.**

To make the mousse, remove the base from the refrigerator and in a mixer fitted with the whisk attachment, whip the white chocolate cream on medium-low speed into fluffy, soft peaks, 2 to 3 minutes. (Be careful not to overwhip it or the mixture will separate.)

To serve, place small dabs of the white chocolate mousse in the center of 4 dessert plates (to use as glue). Place a shard of phyllo on each dab of mousse and then place a spoonful of mousse on top of the phyllo. Repeat with 2 more phyllo shards and spoonfuls of mousse, and then dust with powdered sugar.

To make the white chocolate cream base for the mousse, put the chocolate in a medium bowl. In a small saucepan, heat the cream over medium heat until it just comes to the boil. Immediately turn off the heat and pour the hot cream over the white chocolate, whisking until the chocolate is melted and smooth. Add the grape-fruit zest. Cover and refrigerate overnight.*

Preheat the oven to 350°F. Line a cookie sheet with parchment paper and set aside.

To make the chocolate phyllo, in a small bowl, stir the cocoa with the warm melted butter. Place a sheet of phyllo on the parchment-lined cookie sheet and spatter it then brush it with the cocoa–butter mixture. Sprinkle evenly with 2 tablespoons of the sugar and then place another phyllo sheet on top. Spatter and brush with the cocoa–butter mixture, sprinkle with 2 tablespoons more sugar, and repeat the process 2 more times so you end up with 4 layers ending with sugar. Cover the stacked phyllo with parchment paper and place another baking sheet on top of the parchment to weight it down and keep the phyllo from buckling during baking. (If your cookie sheet has a rim then you may need to use a smaller pan as a top sheet for weighting.)

continued on page 78

easy **white chocolate–grapefruit mousse** with chocolate phyllo

MAKES 4 SERVINGS

One of Julia Child's more remarkable traits was her never-ending quest for knowledge. This iconic woman, who taught several generations how to cook and appreciate good food, was never afraid to ask questions and was always eager to learn something new. When I was filming at her house for her series on baking, she asked *me* how I work with phyllo dough, so I showed her this recipe. Layers of crispy phyllo, painted with a mixture of cocoa powder and butter, make the perfect "bread" for this stacked dessert club sandwich. The filling is a super easy grapefruit-spiked white chocolate mousse.

| do-aheads |
*The white chocolate cream must be made 24 hours before you want to serve the dessert and can be kept for as long as 48 hours.

**The phyllo shards can be kept in an airtight container at room temperature for up to 4 days.

| you'll need |
2 cookie sheets
Parchment paper

for the white chocolate–grapefruit mousse
6 ounces white chocolate, chopped

1½ cups heavy cream

1 teaspoon grated grapefruit zest

Powdered sugar, for serving

for the chocolate phyllo
¼ cup cocoa powder

8 tablespoons (1 stick) unsalted butter, melted and warm

4 sheets phyllo dough

½ cup sugar

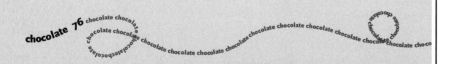

white chocolate **sherbet**

MAKES ABOUT 1 QUART, OR 8 SERVINGS

Serve this delicious spiked white chocolate sherbet with ripe, bursting-with-flavor berries. Raspberries are particularly nice because their slight tartness is a natural foil to the sweetness of the white chocolate.

Have ready near your cooktop a large bowl filled three-quarters full with ice and add enough water to cover the ice.

In a medium saucepan, bring the milk, water, vanilla bean, and sugar almost to a boil. Turn off the heat and whisk in the white chocolate until it's melted. Strain through a fine-mesh sieve into a bowl and then place the bowl in the larger bowl of ice water. Stir occasionally until the mixture has chilled, about 10 minutes.*

Pour the mixture into the bowl of an ice cream maker and freeze the sherbet according to the ice cream maker's instructions. Transfer to a container with a lid and freeze for at least 2 hours.**

do-aheads

*The sherbet base can be made 2 days ahead and refrigerated.

**The sherbet is best served the same day it's made, but it can be kept frozen for 3 days. Let it soften slightly at room temperature for 10 minutes before serving if it seems too hard.

you'll need

Ice cream maker

1½ cups whole milk

⅔ cup water

1 vanilla bean, halved lengthwise or 1 tablespoon vanilla bean paste

1 tablespoon sugar

8 ounces white chocolate, chopped

for the white chocolate filling

3 ounces white chocolate

3 ounces cream cheese, at room
temperature

3 tablespoons unsalted butter,
softened

To make the filling, melt the chocolate in a heat-proof bowl set over (but not touching) a pan of simmering water. Set aside to cool slightly.

In a mixer fitted with the paddle attachment, beat the cream cheese with the butter until light and fluffy, about 5 minutes. With the mixer running, drizzle in the white chocolate and stir until blended. Transfer to a clean pastry bag fitted with a medium ($\frac{1}{4}$-inch) plain tip.

Make the sandwiches by piping an $\frac{1}{8}$-inch layer of white chocolate filling onto the flat sides of half of the cookies. Lightly press the flat sides of the unfrosted ones to the frosted ones.✶✶

$\frac{1}{2}$ cup powdered sugar and whip until the whites hold stiff peaks. Using a rubber spatula, gently fold in a third of the almond mixture, letting some streaks remain. Fold in the remaining almond mixture in 2 batches, just until barely combined; the batter will be rather soupy.

Place a medium ($\frac{1}{4}$-inch) plain tip in a large pastry bag. Put the pastry bag (with a clothes pin holding the bottom closed) in a tall container such as an empty coffee can or vase. Fold over the open end of the pastry bag to make it easier to fill, and fill with the almond batter.

On parchment-lined cookie sheets, pipe rows of 1-inch kisses (about the size of a quarter) $1\frac{1}{2}$ inches apart. Let the piped cookies sit at room temperature for 30 minutes to dry out slightly and form a skin. Bake one pan at a time for 17 minutes, or until the cookies are a very light brown, rotating the back of the pan to the front after 8 minutes so the cookies bake evenly.

Immediately after removing the pans from the oven and while the cookies are still hot, spoon a tablespoon of water under one end of the parchment and tip the pan slightly to make the water seep under the paper. This will steam the cookies loose. Let the cookies cool completely before peeling them off the paper.*

continued on page 74

chocolate "burgers" with
white chocolate filling

MAKES ABOUT 15 SANDWICH COOKIES

When I go to Paris to visit my French friend Muriel (I call her Murf), who I've known since college, we always make it a point to have tea on the Place de la Madeleine and then stop for traditional French macaroons at Ladurée. The ones I love are made into small sandwich cookies and come in all sizes and pastel colors. Lined up in their glass case in Paris, they look like jewels waiting to be bought and worn. Once I'm back in the States in my own kitchen, they look more like little hamburgers, so on Tru's dessert cart I affectionately call them "burgers." The white chocolate filling recipe here makes a little more than you'll need, but extra is good spread on top of cupcakes or graham crackers or sandwiched between ladyfingers or vanilla wafers.

Preheat the oven to 300°F.

To make the chocolate macaroons, in a bowl, stir together the almond flour, cocoa powder, and 2½ cups of the powdered sugar until combined. Sift through a medium-mesh sieve to remove any large pieces of almond.

In a mixer fitted with the whisk attachment, whip the egg white on medium speed until frothy. Add the remaining

| do-aheads |

*The cookies can be made up to 1 week ahead and kept in an airtight container.

**The filled cookies can be kept in the refrigerator for up to 5 days. Let come to room temperature before serving.

| you'll need |

Parchment paper

Cookie sheet

Large pastry bag with a medium (¼-inch) plain tip

for the "buns" (chocolate macaroons)

- 5 tablespoons almond flour or ground almonds
- ½ tablespoon cocoa powder, preferably Dutch-processed
- 3 cups powdered sugar
- 1 large egg white

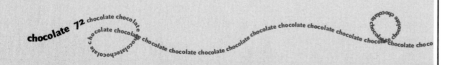

Lightly dust a work surface with flour and turn the dough out onto it. Knead the dough by hand 5 to 10 times, just enough to form the dough into a smooth ball.* Dust more flour on the work surface and, using a rolling pin, roll the dough out into a ¼-inch-thick square about 8 inches by 8 inches. Transfer the dough to the parchment-lined cookie sheet by rolling it up around the rolling pin and then unrolling it onto the paper. Roll the dough a little bit more once it's on the cookie sheet to make it slightly thinner (it's easier to transfer the dough when it's thicker). Using a fork, prick the surface of the dough all over to prevent any buckling or shrinkage. I like to entwine 2 forks to make it go more quickly. Put the pan in the refrigerator to chill for 30 minutes.**

Preheat the oven to 350°F.

Remove the pan from the refrigerator and, using a sharp knife (to cut cleanly through the currants), trim the dough so the edges are straight, then cut the dough into 2-inch squares. Place them 1 inch apart on the cookie sheet.

Bake for 15 minutes. Remove any air pockets by knocking the pan once against the oven rack, and then rotate the pan to ensure it cooks evenly. Bake for 10 to 15 minutes more, until the shortbread is light gold in color. Remove from the oven and let the shortbread cool in the pan for 30 minutes.

Put the white chocolate in a bowl set over (but not touching) a saucepan of less than barely simmering water. Stir once or twice until it's evenly melted. Dip a corner of each of the short-bread squares in the chocolate so the chocolate coats one side diagonally from corner to corner. Shake them slightly as you remove them to shake off any excess chocolate. Place the dipped shortbread back on the parchment paper for the chocolate to cool and set up.***

white chocolate–dipped
currant shortbread

MAKES 16 PIECES

I love the buttery, "short," melt-in-your-mouth texture of this shortbread and the contrast of the chewy petite dried currants and white chocolate. It's teatime!

Line a cookie sheet with parchment and set aside.

In a mixer fitted with the paddle attachment, beat the butter on medium speed until light and fluffy, 3 to 5 minutes. Add the sugar and mix until it's incorporated into the butter. In a bowl, stir the flour together with the cornstarch and salt, and then add to the butter mixture. Mix on low speed until the ingredients are almost combined, then add the currants and mix just until the dough begins to come together.

| do-aheads |

*The dough can be made and refrigerated for 2 days or frozen, well-wrapped, for up to 2 months before rolling out.

**The dough can be rolled, placed on the cookie sheet, rolled again, and kept covered in the refrigerator for up to 2 days.

***The shortbreads will keep for 1 week in an airtight container.

| you'll need |
Parchment paper
Cookie sheet

8 tablespoons (1 stick) unsalted butter, cut in ½-inch pieces and softened
¼ cup sugar
1 cup all-purpose flour
¼ cup cornstarch
¼ teaspoon salt
⅓ cup currants
6 ounces white chocolate, chopped

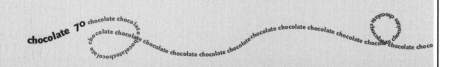

Preheat the oven to 400°F.

Lay half of the graham cracker halves on a cookie sheet. Top each with a dark chocolate square and then a white chocolate square. Place 2 marshmallows side by side on top of the chocolate.

Bake until the marshmallows are puffed and golden brown, 3 to 5 minutes. Remove from the oven and top each with a remaining graham cracker half, pressing down lightly to make a sandwich. Serve immediately, while still warm.

white and dark chocolate

s'mores

MAKES 4 S'MORES

One year at the Fourth of July party my friend Karen and I used to throw annually, I overheard a man saying to a gaggle of children, "You know, you just can't get a perfectly roasted marshmallow anymore." I thought to myself, "There are lots of things I *can't* do, but as a pastry chef, one thing I *can* do is perfectly roast a marshmallow." So off I went to the campfire to prove to him that patience (the key ingredient for perfectly roasted marshmallows) was still in existence somewhere. I presented him with a golden orb of toasted perfection and Jimmy and I have been in love ever since.

The best place, in my opinion, to put a gooey hot marshmallow is with two squares of chocolate sandwiched between graham crackers. My preference is for white and dark chocolate in my s'mores, but if you prefer, substitute milk chocolate. If you have a campfire or fireplace available, roast your marshmallows (patiently) the old-fashioned way. I've devised the following recipe for the oven, and for bakers with less time.

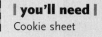

| you'll need |
Cookie sheet

4 whole graham crackers, broken into 8 halves

½ (1.55-ounce) dark chocolate bar, broken into 4 squares

½ (1.55-ounce) white chocolate bar, broken into 4 squares

8 large marshmallows

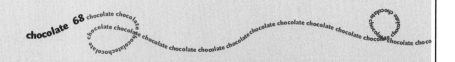

In a large bowl, whisk the egg yolks with the granulated sugar until just combined. Whisking constantly, gradually pour in the warm cream mixture. If using vanilla extract, whisk it in now. Strain through a fine-mesh sieve into the smaller baking pan.

Put the filled baking pan, still set into the larger dish, into the oven. Pour the boiling water into the large dish until it comes halfway up the side of the smaller pan. Bake for 40 to 50 minutes, or until the custard just seems set but still shimmies a little in the center (it will continue to cook and thicken as it cools).

Remove the pan from the water and let cool for 15 minutes. Tightly cover with plastic wrap, making sure the plastic does not touch the custard. Refrigerate for at least 3 hours.*

To serve, scoop rounded spoonfuls of the custard and smooth the surfaces a little with a small spatula or butter knife, letting them remain rounded on top. Put the spoons of custard on a cookie sheet and return to the refrigerator to chill for 30 minutes before caramelizing the surface.**

Position a rack 6 inches from the broiling element and heat a broiler to its highest heat setting (or have a kitchen torch ready).

Sprinkle a layer of coarse sugar over the surface of each spoonful of custard so they're entirely covered. Place under the broiler until the sugar is melted and golden brown, usually less than a minute. Alternatively, caramelize the sugar with a torch. Let cool for 1 minute before serving. (Make sure the spoon handles are cool before picking them up.)